Contemporary Problems of Drug Abuse

Contemporary Problems of Drug Abuse

Edited by Peter A. Levin

PUBLISHING SCIENCES GROUP, INC.
ACTON, MASSACHUSETTS

Printed in the United States of America.

International Standard Book Number: 0-88416-002-5

Library of Congress Catalog Card Number: 73-84168

Contents

Foreword

A sometimes disconcerting but always challenging thing happened at the Villanova University School of Law last March. For two days and nights hundreds of students of both law and medicine met and participated in a national symposium on the "Contemporary Problems of Drug Abuse."

The symposium took place because Peter A. Levin, a former student and now an assistant district attorney in Philadelphia, thought that it should. The announcement prepared for the symposium stated its purpose in simple terms: "to provide law and medical students with the basic framework of knowledge they will need to develop expertise in the area of drug abuse. It is hoped that participants will gain a deeper understanding of their professional responsibilities as well as a certain amount of hard technical data concerning drug abuse."

What followed was anything but simple. National and local, legal and medical authorities, films, and small theater groups were combined to create a constantly changing forum which demanded the attention of all those present. Ideas, notions, perceptions, and judgments, some firm and some vague, were attacked with enthusiasm. The panel members were informed, interested, and articulate.

Nothing can recreate the intense, often personal, debates of those days and nights, but this book, an edited transcript, will allow you to share in that very fine, sometimes disconcerting, but always challenging thing that happened here last March.

J. Willard O'Brien
Dean, Villanova University
July 27, 1973 · · · · · · · · · · · · · · · · School of Law

Acknowledgments

I am grateful to Glenn Gilman and Michael Gold who assisted me in the development of the symposium and to our staff consisting of Michael Berkowitz, Peter Bowers, Gene Castellano, Warren Lassin, Joseph McGill, Jo Ann Moldawer, Don Sanders, and James Schwartz. Without the help of these individuals the symposium would never have been possible. I also express sincere appreciation to Villanova Law School, its faculty, its Law Review, and the Student Bar Association for their cooperation and able assistance.

This symposium was financially supported in part by grants from: Abbott Laboratories; American Bar Association's Drug Abuse Education Program (Young Lawyers Section); Bell Telephone Company of Pennsylvania; Ciba-Geigy Corporation; First Pennsylvania Bank; First Pennsylvania Charitable Foundation; Hellwig, Inc.; Ives Laboratories, Lakeside Laboratories; The Legal Intelligencer; Eli Lilly & Company; McNeil Laboratories, Inc.; Merck Sharp & Dohme; Merrell-National Laboratories; Rapid-National Graphic Services, Inc.; A. H. Robbins Company; Roche Laboratories; Sandoz-Wander, Inc.; Schering Corporation; Smith, Kline & French Laboratories; United Fund Torch Drive; Upjohn Company; Villanova Law School Student Bar Association.

Peter A. Levin

Chapter 1

Introduction

Ultimately, lawyers and doctors are the ones who must deal with the contemporary problems of drug use and abuse. The difficulties encountered in this sensitive area are often complicated further because they must work in an arena of conflicting data and unyielding myths.

In light of the pressing need for lawyers and doctors to develop greater understanding and expertise in this area, the 1973 symposium, "Contemporary Problems of Drug Abuse," was sponsored by the American Medical Association and the American Bar Association. Representing the first large-scale, nationwide educational effort aimed at the legal and medical professions, the symposium revealed concern for the problems of drug abuse at various levels, from law enforcement and reform to the physical and psychological consequences of drug use and abuse.

The Authors

Peter A. Levin
Contemporary Problems of Drug Abuse

Mr. Levin is a specialist in drug rehabilitation and education programs in the Philadelphia District Attorney's Office. He also serves as criminal justice co-ordinator for the Coordinating Office for Drug and Alcohol Abuse Programs of Philadelphia, as a consultant to the Treatment Alternatives to Street Crime Program (TASC), and is Pennsylvania chairman for the American Bar Asso-

1

ciation's Drug Abuse Education Project. He conducted a pilot program in drug abuse law at Villanova Law School.

Robert W. Meserve
Drug Abuse and the Role of ABA

Mr. Meserve, an attorney serving as counsel to the Boston firm of Nutter, McClennen & Fish, is currently the president of the American Bar Association. A graduate of Tufts College and Harvard Law School, he was active in ABA before assuming the presidency. He has served as an assistant United States attorney for Boston and as a lecturer in law at Harvard Law School and Boston College Law School.

Richard E. Palmer
Drug Abuse and the Role of AMA

Dr. Palmer, a pathologist from Alexandria, Virginia, is presently serving on the American Medical Association's Board of Trustees as secretary-treasurer. He obtained his A.B. and M.D. at The George Washington University where he is now associate clinical professor at the School of Medicine. He is chairman of the Board of Commissioners of the Joint Commission on Accreditation of Hospitals and is pathologist to the Office of the Chief Medical Examiner of Virginia.

Contemporary Problems of Drug Abuse

PETER A. LEVIN

The growing problems associated with drug use and abuse place a special responsibility on today's lawyers and doctors. For the most part, they must make the final decisions concerning persons who are involved with drugs; they must know the differences among drugs, the reasons for their use, and the various treatment modalities available. They are expected to know these things even though most authorities cannot agree on them.

Conflicting Data

A lawyer turns to the medical field for a candid opinion on marihuana and hears that marihuana causes brain damage and leads to heroin use; he is satisfied with this answer until other medical authorities tell him that marihuana causes no physical or psychological harm. Another attorney then asks the medical profession about heroin and is told that heroin causes criminal behavior and is physiologically and psychologically damaging; he feels that this is the answer until he learns that other medical authorities believe heroin causes less organic damage to the body or brain than alcohol, and that many addicts could function normally if given a steady supply of good quality drugs.

A doctor looks for reasons why a person uses drugs, and he gets conflicting data. Psychologists tell the doctor that there are individuals who have "addictive personalities," who are prone to addiction, and who are prone to readdiction after they have been "cured." In this situation, the user's personality has to be totally restructured.

But sociologists do not agree with that theory and tell the doctor that society creates addicts, and causes them to relapse into addiction again. The sense of defeat and hopelessness among slum dwellers, the sense of impotence to effect change, the needs of people to belong to a group—these are the factors that cause addiction, according to sociologists; and, thus, if the addict returns to his same neighborhood, he will become readdicted.

The biochemist tells the doctor that after a person uses heroin a few times the opiate molecule has a direct effect on his nervous system, which adjusts to its presence and becomes dependent upon it. Thus, biochemists would have us believe that a chemical imbalance in the system causes addiction.

Treatment

Not being sure of the drugs themselves or the reasons why persons use them, attorneys and doctors have to determine what to do with the person who comes to them with a drug problem. They are aware that existing treatment for drug abuse has not produced impressive results. They hear that only a small fraction of those addicted to heroin are ever "cured." They hear claims of success and failure in various treatment modalities, but these claims—pro and con—are disputed and largely unsubstantiated.

There is no satisfactory way an attorney or doctor can evaluate the various treatment approaches for different types of drug users. Most treatment programs have relatively narrow data collection and evaluation components, and evaluation among the various programs is impossible because there is no standardized method of doing so. Attorneys and doctors soon learn that all treatment centers have selective admission criteria and do not handle the most criminally active and hard-core addicts.

Crime and Addiction

Judges have even more difficult problems in this regard. A judge has a choice of sending a drug addict to jail or placing him in treatment. Some authorities argue that if an addict is placed in jail, he will not be able to obtain narcotics (or at least not as readily as on the outside). Therefore, when he is released from jail, he will not use drugs again. But the judge hears that ninety-five per cent of the heroin addicts who leave prison relapse immediately. Thus, many judges prefer to place the individual into treatment.

A judge faces an even harder decision with respect to the person who, because he has a drug problem, commits a crime against another person or against property. Shoplifting, prostitution, and sales of drugs are common addict crimes, but so, too, are robberies, burglaries, larcenies, and homicides. Criminal activity relating to narcotics addiction forces thousands of narcotic users into the nation's criminal justice system each year. The need to maintain an expensive habit causes an addict to deal in drugs, to engage in consensual crime, or to steal. It has been estimated that over fifty per cent of all the property crimes in major cities are committed by addicts. And it is further estimated that the citizens of major cities suffer a loss of over $450 million per year in property losses attributed to thefts by addicts. There are also the costs of police, courts, corrections, and parole and probation. Studies have shown that almost all heroin addicts get arrested at least once every two years of active addiction and spend an average of fifteen per cent of their addicted life in jail. Over sixty per cent of those in most prison populations have drug problems.

In spite of the high correlation between crime and addiction, being an addict in and of itself is not a crime. In 1962 the United States Supreme Court ruled that addiction was not a criminal act but rather was to be viewed as a disease. Furthermore, the Court stated that the addict ought to be the object of legitimate programs of treatment and rehabilitation. But many civil libertarians argue that since treatment is largely ineffective, it results in greater punishment in some instances than a prison sentence; and some complain that we do not make exceptions for the problems of other individuals who commit crimes, so why should we make an exception for the person who commits a crime because he is a drug addict. All of these issues confront the judge as he tries to make an appropriate decision.

Education

Law and medical schools, by and large, have not provided adequate training for all of these problems. The 1973 symposium, "Contemporary Problems of Drug Abuse," was the first large-scale, nationwide educational effort aimed at our nation's future lawyers and doctors. Its purpose was to provide law and medical students with the basic framework of knowledge they will need to develop expertise in the area of drug abuse. The undertaking was dedicated to the belief that drug use and abuse is of sufficient importance to warrant this educational effort by the American Bar Association and the American Medical Association.

Drug Abuse and the Role of ABA

ROBERT W. MESERVE

The American Bar Association, as the pre-eminent national organization of the legal profession, is vitally interested in the question of drug abuse, and, through its Law Student Division, participated in the sponsorship of the symposium, "Contemporary Problems of Drug Abuse."

There is no locality where the problem of drug abuse has not come to the attention of men and women in the legal profession. Lawyers become involved with drug abuse either professionally as defenders or prosecutors of individuals charged with drug-related offenses, or as advisers, parents, or citizens.

Legal Responses

Drug abuse and drug addiction present the lawyer with a full range of problems. There are the immediate and practical problems of participating in the law enforcement and criminal justice systems, areas which today are confused at best. The tremendous diversity of statutory sentences for various drug offenses is indicative of the equally great diversity of both legal and public opinion concerning these offenses. Possession of certain drugs is punishable by a fine of five dollars in some jurisdictions and by ten or more years imprisonment in others. We know that use of some drugs—alcohol, for example—constitutes a statistically normal condition in some segments of society, while nothing produces a more violent or hostile reaction in others.

Similarly, confusion also dominates another level at which the lawyer must cope with these issues—the level of law reform. Here, the lawyer functions both as a technician and as a leader. Although we can say with assurance that the present legal response to drug use is irrational, we cannot with equal certainty describe what a rational response would be. Perhaps the most disquieting aspect of our list is the marked lack of unanimity among members of the medical profession concerning the long-term medical consequences of drug use or the physiological and psychological relation of one drug to another. We know that the existence and enforcement of drug control laws may result in other crimes, but we really do not know what we get in return for this social cost. The analogy to prohibition is both attractive and perhaps dangerous or simplistic in that important differences may be obscured, but perhaps it illustrates some of the issues that must be confronted.

Finally, on the jurisprudential level, where the lawyer becomes a philosopher, the fundamental questions of man's relation to man and to society arise. To what extent may society properly prevent an individual from doing something which is harmful to him as an individual, especially when the observed practical result of such a process may or may not be to do harm to others?

Lawyers, by training, solve problems, and there is no reason why the many problems relating to the use and abuse of drugs cannot be solved eventually. Clearly, much more information must be obtained. Since the legal and medical professions have much to offer each other in this regard, the symposium, "Contemporary Problems of Drug Abuse," was an obvious and highly useful undertaking.

Cooperation

The cooperation of medical and law professions in this area has an important precedent. The Young Lawyers Section of the American Bar Association, in cooperation with young doctors all over the country, has sponsored an educational program on the medical and legal consequences of drug use, designed for junior and senior high school students. Teams of doctors and lawyers have presented this program to tens of thousands of students. It has been supported by the voluntary time contributions of hundreds of young professionals, and by a grant from the Law Enforcement Assistance Administration.

When the majority of Americans lived in small communities, the doctor and the lawyer were the natural leaders. Their status rested on their ability to deal with the problems that people had. To maintain that professional status and to fulfill the obligations to society which our professional privileges impose on us, we must continue to deal with the problems which face mankind today.

The drug-abuse symposium and the prospect of involving law and medical students may go far toward coping with one of the most acute problems of our day.

Drug Abuse and the Role of AMA

RICHARD E. PALMER

Insofar as drug abuse and drug dependence constitute serious medical and public health problems, the American Medical Association (AMA) is, of course, committed both to the dissemination of current reliable information to physicians, medical students, and others in the health professions, and to the encouragement of adequate treatment of drug-dependent persons.

Drug abuse and drug dependence represent a complex social problem. The American Medical Association believes that it is important to undertake meaningful interprofessional dialogue to gain greater insight and to formulate workable approaches to the many issues involved.

ABA–AMA Efforts

The American Medical Association cooperated with the American Bar Association in a number of different projects in the past. The National Interprofessional Code was developed and adopted by both organizations some twenty years ago. Annually, since 1965, the National Medical and Legal Symposium has been sponsored by representatives of the American Medical Association and the American Bar Association, and there is an ongoing liaison committee.

In 1969 the American Bar Association and the American Medical Association issued a Joint Statement of Principles concerning alcoholism, the most serious and widespread of all drug dependencies. In that statement the two groups declared that alcoholism should be regarded as an illness in medical and hospital care insurance contracts and that general hospitals should accept, on a nondiscriminatory basis, patients diagnosed as alcoholics. Moreover, they declared that state and local bar and medical associations should appoint committees to work together on alcoholism problems, especially on new legislation that would provide for treatment rather than punishment of the alcoholic.

AMA Activities

As for the broad spectrum of drug abuse, the American Medical Association's interest dates back in recent years to 1963 when, in association with the National Research Council of the National Academy of Sciences, it issued a paper entitled "Narcotics and Medical Practice." This paper set forth the elements of sound medical practice in the use of morphine and other opiate analgesics in the management of patients with drug dependence of the morphine type. This was in its own way a milestone. It proved to be a major source of information for public and private treatment programs across the country and was used by the then Federal Bureau of Narcotics as the authoritative basis for determining what constituted legitimate medical practice in the use of these drugs.

In 1967, and again in 1971, the paper was reissued in modified form to take into account changing circumstances and the acquisition of new knowledge. It was updated to reflect the acceptance of ambulatory treatment with methadone under certain conditions, and the recognition of methadone maintenance techniques as proper medical practice under certain conditions.

Although drug dependence of the morphine type has been of major significance, the American Medical Association has not neglected other forms of dependence. Beginning in 1969, it published reports on diagnostic and treatment considerations involved in dependence of the barbiturate, amphetamine, hallucinogenic, and cannabis types. Last December it had a conference in Washington, D.C., on an oftentimes neglected aspect of drug dependence—medical complications arising from drug abuse. The conference was concerned not only with infectious diseases such as tetanus and hepatitis, but also with damage to the cardiovascular system, liver and kidneys, lungs, and other organs of the body.

Three other meetings sponsored by the American Medical Association in the drug-abuse area have articulated a social as well as a medical concern. In 1967 it brought together narcotics agents, licensure agents, and representatives of large state and county medical societies in an effort to establish some workable method for more effective liaison between law enforcement and medicine in the drug-abuse field. In 1968 it held a conference devoted to the drug-abuse problem among youth. And in 1972 it met to emphasize the role of medical societies in community programs of prevention, treatment, and rehabilitation.

In 1968, again with the National Research Council, the American Medical Association went on record as being one of the first professional organizations calling for more equitable treatment and penalties in the discretionary handling of persons convicted of possessing marihuana for their personal use. In the statement *Marihuana and Society* the American Medical Association and the National Research Council also termed cannabis a dangerous drug and said its use should be discouraged, even though punishment for its possession should be less harsh and more in keeping with the magnitude of the effects. This position was reinforced by the House of Delegates of the American Medical Association this past December. At that time, it passed a resolution urging that the possession of marihuana for personal use be considered no more than a misdemeanor.

The original American Medical Association, National Research Council suggestions on discretionary handling of marihuana users were applied in the Controlled Substances Act of 1970[1] to first offense convictions for possession of any of these scheduled drugs. The AMA testified many times before committees of both houses of Congress concerning bills which led to the final Act.

Education

Another major concern has been the function of the nation's medical schools in furnishing adequate information in appropriate ways on alcoholism and drug abuse. Two AMA publications, *The Manual on Alcoholism* and *Drug Dependence, A Guide for Physicians,* have been distributed free of charge annually to one class in each medical school where they have been requested. In addition, the AMA Council on Mental Health and its Committee on Alcoholism and Drug Abuse or Drug Dependence have established guidelines for instruction on both drug abuse and alcoholism.

1. 21 U.S.C. § 801 (1970).

In a position paper, the council and the committee identified the physician's key role with respect to drug abuse. They called physicians the gatekeepers and their prescription blanks the key for many psychoactive agents. They urged that the education of future physicians encompass the dangers of encouraging or allowing patients to rely upon pills to solve their personal and social problems.

In concluding their paper, the council and the committee had this to say:

> At some time toward the end of their medical school experience, students should have a chance to integrate their various considerations of alcohol and drug use and of abuse. Such integration could be provided through a variety of individual and group experiences, including participation in research projects, preparing papers on literature review, attending specific case conferences, participating in optional or required seminar-type discussions, assuming some responsibility for education about alcoholism and about drug abuse, and participating in preventive and therapeutic programs.

Whatever activities are chosen, they should be designed to integrate the student's total knowledge and understanding.

AMA Objectives

The American Medical Association will continue to work with medicine, with other concerned professionals, and with public officials to evolve better mechanisms for curtailing the abuse of drugs and for dealing intelligently and compassionately with the consequences of drug-abuse.

Chapter 2

Responses

Few disagree with the general goal established in response to drug problems: the reduction of drug abuse and its social cost to society; but disagreements abound when specifics are considered.

The need to apply and regulate human and monetary resources in pursuing goals at the federal level has led to the creation of the Special Action Office. Here, a variety of treatment approaches have been developed, and the number of programs funded by the federal government has grown substantially.

The task of informing the public of risks and consequences of drug use has been difficult, and evaluation of information techniques has been inadequate. The realization that education is not synonymous with prevention has added to disappointments in this area.

If progress is to be made, inconsistencies in response to drug use must not prevent continued efforts to minimize harmful effects. In spite of differences, most who have seriously considered the problems of drug use agree that each drug has its own requirements in terms of availability control, public education, and treatment. Final responses, however, must inevitably pass the test of acceptance by society.

The Author

Jerome H. Jaffe
Responses to Drug-Abuse Problems

Dr. Jaffe was appointed by President Nixon on June 17, 1971, to serve as director of the Special Action Office for Drug Abuse Prevention in the Executive Office of the president, and as special consultant to the president for Narcotics and Dangerous Drugs. Before assuming that position, he served as director of the Drug Abuse Program of the Department of Mental Health of the State of Illinois, as well as associate professor in the Department of Psychiatry at the University of Chicago.

Responses to Drug-Abuse Problems

JEROME H. JAFFE

Our society, like every other society, responds to the use of drugs in a variety of ways, ranging from attempts to control their availability to providing treatment for those who develop drug-related problems. Inasmuch as all our responses are part of a dynamic interreacting process, we have to understand that process to be able to design a rational response. Yet, we all recognize that such an understanding is not sufficient without a clear-cut articulation of our goals. Of course, an articulation of goals is not just a matter of science and technology, but includes values, attitudes, and beliefs. Moreover, our society, like most highly industrialized societies, is one where values, attitudes, and beliefs are continuously changing.

Goals

We can all agree on the most general of goals—the reduction of drug abuse and its social cost to society. However, there is considerable disagreement when we become specific. Some believe that we need stricter penalties; others believe that we only need more research; some believe that we only need treatment; and a few believe that the lowest social cost occurs with total availability of all drugs. It is apparent that we have to be careful in setting goals so that those we pursue in one area do not impinge upon goals we are trying to achieve in others. We should also avoid setting goals that we cannot achieve. Unfortunately, at some point decisions have to be made about the effectiveness of these approaches, so that human and monetary resources can be optimally allocated to achieve some set of goals. The act of looking carefully at the effectiveness of various approaches is a relatively recent development, at least as far as the federal government is concerned.

The Past

Historically, the federal effort was directed almost entirely at what we might think of as the "supply-demand" equation. It was at least twenty years between the time that the Harrison Act[2] was passed to control the availability of drugs and the time the first two federal hospitals to treat drug-dependent people were built at Lexington and Fort Worth. During the next thirty years, these two hospitals represented the entire federal response in terms of treatment, training, education, and research. Then, in 1966 Congress passed the Narcotic Addict Rehabilitation Act,[3] which created a federal civil commitment program, and authorized the funding of a few pilot programs for treatment of narcotics on a voluntary basis in the community. In the summer of 1967, the Office of Economic Opportunity was given funds with which to initiate these programs.

2. Act of Dec. 17, 1914, ch. 1, § 1, 38 Stat. 785.
3. Narcotic Addict Rehabilitation Act of 1966, 80 Stat. 1438 (codified in scattered sections of 18, 28, 42 U.S.C.).

In retrospect, while it seems that the response lagged behind the recognition of a growing problem, until the 1960s, most medical treatment was viewed as a private, local, and state responsibility.

In 1969 there was a further increase in resources for nonlaw enforcement activities. Other federal agencies began to develop programs to deal with various aspects of drug abuse, but the problems were often perceived from the viewpoint of each particular agency, with no apparent mechanism for coordination.

As federal support for these "demand" activities, such as treatment, research, education, training, and prevention, began to accelerate, it became apparent that, while a massive outpouring of funds was theoretically laudable, it might accomplish very little without some mechanism to set meaningful priorities and to coordinate the various efforts. To accomplish this task, the Special Action Office was created.

Special Action Office

However, the task of coordination has not been simple. In 1971 more than 114 agencies scattered through at least eight of the major governmental departments were involved. While the Special Action Office is responsible for functions, it is not a funding agency and does not control or manage the various programs directly. It seems to have been delegated the responsibility without necessarily having the needed authority.

When the Special Action Office was first created, it was obvious that it would have to choose between mobilization and coordination. In June of 1971, it was faced with a number of difficult problems; one was the problem of heroin use among military personnel in Vietnam. Some observers estimated that fifteen to twenty per cent of all servicemen were addicted to heroin; another was the apparent phenomenal gap in the United States between the availability of treatment for drug-dependence problems and the demand for treatment. As far as could be ascertained, 30,000 narcotics users were actively seeking treatment but were unable to get it. In order to understand fully the significance of that figure, you must appreciate the large effort that goes into the development of a treatment program. For example, a program was started in Illinois in 1967 The planning itself took several months. While the program opened in 1968, it was not until three and a half years later, by June 1971, that it finally got 2,000 persons into treatment.

Treatment Approaches

By 1971 the federal government had developed programs sufficient to treat only 16,000 persons at any given time. Therefore, in June 1971, faced with problems of the military, problems of the Veterans Administration, and with at least 30,000 persons waiting for treatment, the Special Action Office set as a primary priority the availability of treatment.

The wide range of drug-abuse problems and the diversity among individuals who at some point require a form of treatment made the Office realize that no single treatment or intervention approach would be adequate. Instead, they pursued a policy of developing a variety of treatment approaches, each, of course, with its own special advantages and disadvantages; each emphasizing one role of treatment over another; and each appealing, perhaps, to somewhat different groups within a heterogeneous population of drug users and addicts.

Some treatment approaches are more controversial than others, for example, the use of synthetic narcotics such as methadone in the treatment of chronic heroin addicts, or the use of civil commitment and other involuntary approaches. The maintenance approach may be necessary for some long-term narcotics addicts, at least as an interim step toward full recovery. However, it is vital that this approach not be used indiscriminately, without concern for the hazards caused by illicit diversion of methadone from treatment programs. Over the past year the Special Action Office has worked very hard to develop new regulations that will minimize those hazards without interfering with treatment; it has also launched new research efforts that, if successful, will further reduce the hazards. Eventually, nonvoluntary approaches to treatment may be required for at least selected groups of addicts, such as those who will accept treatment in lieu of prosecution for crimes committed. However, the Office continues to advocate maximum expansion of voluntary treatment before the investment of substantial resources in nonvoluntary treatment programs.

Significantly, the different approaches to the drug user are not equally effective. We accept the proposition that it is the responsibility of government to determine the reasons for these differences in outcome and efficiency and where appropriate, to redirect federal resources. A massive evaluation effort is now under way because the uncertainties clearly exist and the confusion is real. The evaluation should produce, initially, a careful assessment of the effectiveness of different kinds of treatment. However, it may be some time before there are definitive answers. Until data indicates that a different emphasis is required, the Office will continue to make a variety of treatments available for those who desire treatment, and will continue to invest in the development of more effective treatment methods. This general policy has already resulted in a multimodality treatment system for the country as a whole.

All treatment approaches funded directly by the federal government have grown dramatically; during the past eighteen months, we have developed more treatment capacity than in the previous fifty years. We are now treating more than 60,000 persons at any given time, the equivalent of more than 100,000 on an annual basis. Additionally, many more thousands are treated in programs funded indirectly by the federal government through block grants and other revenue-sharing devices. The combined federal, state, local, and private capacity is now estimated at more than 120,000 persons at any given time, the equivalent of an annual capacity of more than 200,000.

The Special Action Office is committed to continue the expansion of treatment programs until no one can say that he committed a crime to get drugs because there was no treatment available. The achievement of that goal is contingent only upon a commitment on the part of state and local governments to continue their present levels of support.

There will be many accused of minor crimes or of simple possession of drugs whose willingness to consider treatment may not develop until they are arrested. A model program—Treatment Alternatives to Street Crimes (TASC)—has been developed that will link the criminal justice system more closely to the network of treatment and rehabilitation programs. The purpose of TASC is to identify drug users at the point of arrest. If ordinarily those individuals would be released pending trial, this linkage would permit them to be admitted directly into treatment programs. Since these programs are essentially local, the practices vary. In some programs, entering and remaining in treatment may be a condition of release. In others, progress in treatment may be considered heavily in a decision to prosecute or to sentence.

Generally, preventive efforts should flow from an understanding of the causes of drug use and of excessive drug use. However, with the exception of controlling drug availability, there is very little consensus about which of the many factors associated either with drug experimentation or excessive drug use can be modified.

Educational Efforts

Further, informing the public of the risks and consequences of drug use is a responsibility of government at all levels as well as that of other social institutions. But if conveying knowledge about possible adverse effects has had any substantial impact on the rate of experimentation or addiction, the impact is clearly inadequate.

Unfortunately, many educational efforts do not have clearly articulated goals, and few of the efforts relying on communication of information, whether through school systems, social institutions, or mass media, have been rigorously evaluated. Where evaluation has been attempted, the data do not show significant impact. The Office intends to refocus efforts on providing creative pilot preventive approaches with more clearly articulated goals, which will be designed in ways that will permit objective evaluation.

All too often, films, pamphlets, brochures, posters, and television spot announcements remain unevaluated in terms of their impact on various target audiences. The federal government has instructed all agencies to stop direct production and support of new educational and mass media materials relating to drug abuse until the impact of presently available material can be better assessed. This, of course, is going to require the development of the technology capable of assessing these activities; efforts aimed at this development are being made.

It is also clear that education is not synonymous with prevention—either prevention of initial experimentation or prevention of the progression on to heavy use and addiction. In some situations, the most effective way to reduce the social cost of drug use is to provide meaningful alternatives. Other effective approaches have involved early intervention efforts aimed at bringing drug users into treatment before drug use progresses to addiction or becomes incorporated into the individual's values.

Availability

There is one factor that most persons agree is related to drug use, namely, availability. Moreover, this is the one factor that society has traditionally expected government to control, and government at all levels has, in fact, devoted considerable energy to this effort. However, there are now some individuals who feel that this approach is inappropriate and is emphasized too much. This creates an interesting paradox, because some of the groups that are saying there is too much emphasis on law enforcement and drug-abuse control are the same groups that are advocating that new drugs, such as barbiturates, amphetamines, and other sedatives, be brought into the same control system.

Until 1969 the federal government's response to demands was pitifully small. It has, however, increased each year since 1969. In moving toward the primary goal of making treatment available, the budget for treatment of drug abuse and related activities has gone from $42 million in 1969 to $419 million for fiscal year 1974.

Yet many persons have now voiced concern about a possible overresponse—overresponse even on the part of treatment. Only time will tell if that money is well spent. At present, we need not apologize for expending funds to increase the availability of treatment, to increase research, and to increase the capacity of states to make more of these decisions.

Attitudes

Most critics recommend what all of us want—bold innovation, but without mistakes; and rapid expansion, but with certain efficiency and effectiveness. Those who know the nature of institutions recognize that we cannot have both rapid expansion and simultaneous careful evaluation.

It has become increasingly common for every symposium to have at least one speaker who feels it is necessary to tell those in attendance that they are idiots for showing concern for any drug other than alcohol. Alcohol is indeed a major problem, a problem with a horrendous social cost, but it is not being ignored. In fact, there are programs for alcoholism in both the Veterans Administration and in the Department of Defense. Moreover, the private sector has multiple programs devoted to treatment and prevention of alcoholism, as do state and local governments. There is an entire institute within the National Institute of Mental Health devoted solely to the problem of this drug—alcohol. Therefore, you should consider alcohol and its problems as you discuss other drugs that our society uses, but you should also recognize that there is a certain illogic about an exclusive focus on it.

The history and the nature of nonmedical drug use is such that the medical and social consequences of using a particular drug do not always correlate with the attitudes and use patterns that develop. Thus, the use of an artificial sweetener that in large doses has a cancer-producing effect in rats is prohibited while the smoking of material that is believed to be responsible for cancer in man is not. Inconsistencies in our over-all response, however, must not be a justification for abandoning all efforts at developing a rational system that seems to minimize the harmful effects of drug use. Neither should the shortcomings of all constructive efforts be used as a reason for abandoning them entirely, as some may advocate. Fortunately, most of us recognize that this is not a realistic approach.

The medical utility and the medical and social consequences of different drugs dictate diverse approaches to their misuse for nonmedical purposes. Thus, the approach to each drug necessarily involves varying degrees of legal regulation and control of availability, as well as varied allocation of resources to the different aspects of the problem, i.e., the enforcement of drug-control laws, the treatment of the adverse consequences of drug use, the public dissemination of information relating to use and abuse, and the development of increased understanding that will help minimize the social costs resulting from the use of any drug in a modern society. No single approach by itself has been able to minimize the social cost of drug use, and it is not likely that any single approach ever will. Indeed, when we examine proposals to improve the situation, we find that most of them represent only a minor tinkering with the system.

Although there are some who advocate that all drugs should be freely available, most who have looked seriously at the problems of drug use recognize that the approach to each different drug requires a different degree of availability control, public education, and treatment.

Much of the disagreement in dealing with the drug problem

centers around the question of how much human energy and concern should be allocated to a particular drug, and to the particular aspect of the effort which is selected to reduce social costs—control of availability or other preventive approaches. There are some who feel that these problems, as they affect the federal government, could be resolved through organizational changes. The Special Action Office was originally intended to have the kind of authority that would permit it to move functions from one agency to another, thus effecting a reorganization over a period of time. That power, unfortunately, was not granted, so that efforts at coordination have taken somewhat longer than anticipated. At present, it has moved most discretionary funds into a single agency, the National Institute for Mental Health (NIMH). In 1969 the discretionary money for drug-abuse prevention activity was spread throughout a dozen agencies, with over sixty-six per cent in NIMH. In 1974 it is expected that virtually ninety per cent of all discretionary resources will be in that single agency.

We should recognize that we are engaged in a dialogue involving more than the pharmacology of drugs. For many, the idea of drug use of any kind runs counter to fundamental values. It is the symbol as much as the substance. Inevitably, proposals about how a society should respond to problems of drug use touch upon what a society should be, and say something about its fundamental values.

It is not likely that there will ever be total agreement among officials and, thus, there will continue to be differences about the role of drug use in society. Yet, we cannot wait until there is consensus. Policies are made, legislators continue to legislate, lawyers continue to litigate, and doctors continue to treat, although there are some who would deny that what they do is needed and others who would claim that what they do is not treatment.

Actions that are put forth as solutions to problems have costs and they have risks. Many of the costs and risks of our actions as a nation were considered at the drug abuse symposium. Ultimately, our responses to drug use must be responses that most of society can live with and accept. It is doubtful whether we will quickly reach consensus, but if we continue to agree to discuss our differences, we shall have come far.

Chapter 3

History

Both the medical and legal professions have contributed to public fear of certain substances, which in turn has prompted regulation or prohibition. Frightening and inaccurate reports were already plentiful by the 1920s and 1930s.

For half a century there was a federal policy against addiction maintenance. Physicians were labeled as the prime cause of American addiction, and in 1919 the Supreme Court excluded addiction maintenance from the practice of medicine; narcotics maintenance clinics were doomed as governmental efforts to curb drug availability took shape.

History has shown that both the medical and legal professions have, like everyone else, often accepted erroneous and passionate judgments. When social disorder and tension are simply attributed to the use of a particular substance, anger, fear, and frustration make it less likely that there can be flexible regulation and reasonable punishment for its use and sale.

The Author

David F. Musto
History of Drug Control
Dr. Musto is assistant professor of history and psychiatry at Yale University. A graduate of Yale University, he received his M.D. from the University of Washington. He serves as a historical consultant to the Special Action Office

of Drug Abuse Prevention and is a fellow at the Drug Abuse Council in Washington, D.C. Dr. Musto is the author of *American Disease: Origins of Narcotic Control.*

History of Drug Control

DAVID E. MUSTO

For more than a century, Americans have sought to control through legal means substances, like morphine, which the medical profession has agreed are hazardous. The cooperation of the medical and legal professions in the regulation or prohibition of certain drugs—opium, cocaine, alcohol, heroin, and cannabis—sheds great light on the role of those institutions in channelling public concern or fear into practical action. Both professions are closely in step with the prevailing current national fear, and are quite capable of reinforcing and implementing what, in hindsight, may appear as a distortion of reality. For example, some of the past events in American drug control, which may now appear inexplicable, can be understood if they are placed in historical context. We must rediscover the powerful reasons for the legal profession's ingenuity with such stumbling blocks as constitutional separation of federal and state powers, and examine the medical profession's often more than occasional willingness to offer conclusions regarding social policy wrapped in its prestige and authority. Those conclusions, ostensibly arising from medical science, are often personal opinions—sincere, to be sure—that were strongly influenced by the same social forces which were simultaneously molding general public opinion, so that they seemed to doctors to be scientific truths.

Some examples of legal and medical cooperation regarding widespread fear of certain substances are given below, along with considerations why such seemingly anomalous events were considered to be in the best interests of the nation, and fully justified in the opinion of the professions' leaders at the time. An examination of the context in which laws were passed, or control decisions made, illuminates the larger question of social control of deviance, of which the control of dangerous substances is a part. The examples provide a historical dimension for considering current recommendations for action.

Antimaintenance

First, consider what was for fifty years the chief characteristic of American drug control—the federal policy against addiction maintenance. In 1919 two crucial Supreme Court decisions— *U.S. v. Doremus*[4] and *Webb* v. *U.S.*[5]—made almost all forms of addiction maintenance illegal. In effect, the decisions took away the physician's right to decide whether an opiate user with no other ailment should or could be maintained in his addictive state. Indeed, the decisions made such practice a considerable hazard to the practitioner. Much obloquy has been heaped on this interpretation of the Harrison Act.[6] As decades have passed, the decisions' historical context has been forgotten and the action appears almost accidental. In recent years some lawyers have concluded that the Supreme Court was "tricked" into outlawing maintenance —perhaps by a cleverly worded appeal brief. It has also been charged that the medical profession was not consulted in 1919, that it was "the lawyers' fault" that we have such a serious problem with opiate abuse, because simple users were made into criminals by uninformed court action. Other critics have regretted that if it were not for these decisions, the United States would have had the benefits of the so-called British system—permitting physicians to use their own judgment regarding addiction maintenance. Since this was explicitly stated in the Rolleston Report of

4. 249 U.S. 86 (1919).
5. 249 U.S. 96 (1919).
6. Act of Dec. 17, 1914, ch. 1, § 1, 38 Stat. 785.

1926, the British system is said to have held down addiction in Great Britain, and even to have reduced drastically the number of addicts. Since antimaintenance is a long-standing core element in the American attitude toward opiate use, it may be useful to inquire whether men not usually thought to be gullible, such as Justices Oliver Wendell Holmes and Louis Brandeis, were indeed tricked by cleverly worded appeals into supporting the move to outlaw addiction maintenance.

Drug Control

There are some actions by the medical profession regarding narcotic control which may appear equally indefensible; consider the testimony of the American Medical Association (AMA) spokesman at the 1924 congressional hearings on the prohibition of heroin manufacture. Dr. Charles Richardson, representative of AMA's Board of Trustees' executive committee, appeared and told the House Committee that: "Heroin contains, physiologically, the double action of cocaine and morphia. It produces the excitation of cocaine, with the sedative action of morphia . . . . [It] de-throne[s] their moral responsibility. It gives them an exalted impression of their own importance, and criminals by using it obtain this result." It was stated that heroin did not just create crime as a result of the cost of the drug on the black-market, but that heroin had a positive stimulating effect toward crime, crime of a most violent and senseless brutality. Dr. Dana Hubbard, another physician and director of public health education at New York City's Health Department, declared at the same hearing that "the physiological effect of heroin is to benumb the inhibitors and make of moral cowards brutal, brainless men, without fear and without conscience. . . . The heroin question is not a medical one, as heroin addicts spring from sin and crime." It is safe to say that these statements were inaccurate and misleading, which is especially disturbing in light of the fact that you would expect the medical profession to be well informed.

Another example arises from the furor over cannabis in the 1930s. The vast majority of medical reports written then described cannabis as far more dangerous than is now assumed. Even those who questioned the generally believed connection between crime and the use of marihuana reported that marihuana, when smoked, released inhibitions to expressions of violence and sexual expression, particularly homosexual desires. Thus, clinical reports favored the strict control of marihuana, which was thought, among other things, to be a potent cause of insanity.

Another example of a leading medical authority who supported fearful and apparently inaccurate reports on drugs was Dr. Edward Huntington Williams. In a 1911 medical journal he described the effects of cocaine as being particularly appealing to blacks, driving them to senseless brutality against whites in the South, and further reported that cocaine improved the marksmanship of users so that almost every shot hit home. As recently as 1965 Dr. Williams was described in a respected study of addiction as a "nationally known expert on narcotic addiction whose writings are still read with respect."

The foregoing are just a few examples of how the medical profession used the language and apparent objectivity of science to confirm already exaggerated fears—both about drugs and the groups that used them. Thus, with regard to fundamental aspects of dangerous substance control we have the legal profession described as either tricked or tricky, and the medical profession described as misleading and uninformed. In order to understand these severe condemnations, must we posit evil intentions, or a conspiracy, or can we learn from these instances something about the usual role, then and now, of medical and legal institutions? It is clear that objectivity about dangers to society can be just as difficult for doctors and lawyers as for anyone else: law and medicine are integral parts of total society and attempt to move with the rest of society, as harmoniously as it is possible.

My own research into the evolution of American narcotic controls does not support the suspicion that these seeming aberrations are to be explained either by a conspiracy theory, or by the assertion that the legal and medical professions are simply self-aggrandizing. The better we understand how institutions, such as medicine and law, are part of the whole society and are only partly independent, the better we can interpret present events and guard against overvaluation of professional opinions. None of us can be free of social pressures and strong currents of popular opinion, and what may now appear reasonable may appear clearly one-sided or distorted to a later generation. Unfortunately, what may be our idiosyncratic beliefs and what counts as an advance over past beliefs are not easy to determine. But certainly we can be more critical of our basic assumptions and self-satisfied attitudes.

Medical Restrictions

By World War I, political reformers and even medical leaders agreed that half of the American addicts, estimated in the millions, had been created by mercenary or poorly trained physicians. It is not surprising, then, that the Court's antimaintenance formulation was seen by many frustrated and knowledgeable reformers as the only way—perhaps the last chance—to counteract the cause of half the "dope fiends" in the nation. Somehow, the federal government had to control the doctors who hid behind their state licenses while selling dope or prescriptions and needlessly addicting patients. For a layman's view of the "dope doctor," and the fearful image of addiction among American families before the Harrison Act of 1914[7] you can look to Eugene O'Neil's autobiographical drama, *Long Day's Journey Into Night*. O'Neil portrays his mother's addiction at the hands of an incompetent doctor as the family's curse and horror. It was in this mood that many Americans wanted to obtain some control over physicians' judgment and practice.

By 1910 it was considered that the states had failed in their

7. *Ibid.*

attempts to control doctors, druggists, and manufacturers. The problem facing constitutional lawyers was how to curb medical and pharmaceutical practice by *federal* law. The right to regulate medical practice was clearly reserved to the states—any infringement was bound to be vigorously contested in the courts. In effect, the Supreme Court decisions of 1919 solved this dilemma by excluding addiction maintenance from the practice of medicine and, therefore, from the exclusive control of the states. To have permitted exceptions, that is, for the Court to say that some doctors could maintain simple addicts but that the wrong type of doctor could not, would have been an obvious attempt to regulate the practice of medicine. As a consequence, the Supreme Court's imposition of control over the professional use of drugs had to have a rigid, dogmatic character to avoid the appearance of licensing the professions. Leaders of the medical and legal professions cooperated to control the group which was considered the prime cause of American addiction: the physicians. Legal ingenuity in overcoming constitutional restrictions and problems, and the determination among the medical profession's leadership that reform was an absolute necessity, led to this rigid formulation—a trade-off which was felt to be, on balance, worth the inconvenience and difficulties it caused. Here is what the president of the American Medical Association said a few months after the 1919 Supreme Court decisions:

> These laws are making it more and more burdensome for physicians using the narcotics legitimately, but that is a mere annoyance. The responsibility on the medical profession is becoming greater and greater to see to it that some action should be taken against a few renegade and depraved members of the profession who, joining with the criminal class, make it possible to continue the evil and illicit drug trade.

Federal Response

What may appear as capricious or ill-informed was in fact a strenuous effort to control, as effectively as then possible, a rise in addiction—considered a national menace. Yet, the Court's decision was close, five to four, with liberal members such as Holmes and Brandeis favoring expansion of federal powers to protect the public, and with other Court members, like the archconservative Justice James Clark McReynolds, believing that the extension of federal policy powers into medical practice was simply and blatantly unconstitutional. The closeness of this landmark decision had a strong effect on the antinarcotic enforcement style of the federal government until fairly recently. Federal antinarcotic agencies had an extreme reluctance, one might say fear, to compromise publicly on the question of maintenance, lest they appear to be regulating medical practice. Maintenance was at times permitted through unofficial understandings between agents and physicians. Formal tolerance of narcotic maintenance clinics became an obvious threat to the federal interpretation of the Harrison Act.[8] The clinics could not publicly and officially dispense narcotics, and still permit indictment of "dope doctors" for the same kind of action. Yet, this was only one reason the clinics were closed; a second reason was that the clinics made narcotics available while the federal government's position had been, from at least 1906 onward, that the drugs should be made scarce and strictly limited to legitimate medical purposes, such as pain relief. Maintenance clinics seemed inconsistent with the campaign to seek international control of narcotics—for example, asking Turkey and Persia to plow under large crops of opium poppies, while simultaneously distributing narcotics from city health departments. Thus, a harmonization of governmental efforts to curb drug availability helped doom the narcotic maintenance clinics.

A similar fate might await methadone programs. One major difference, however, is that the federal government has now, through the evolution of constitutional law, the accepted power to control the prescription of dangerous drugs. As a result, the 1970

8. *Ibid.*

Comprehensive Drug Abuse Prevention and Control Act,[9] based on the power to regulate interstate commerce, enables the federal government to revoke physicians' Controlled Substances Registration Certificates. If this extension of federal powers had been possible in 1919, it is likely that the controls enforced thereafter might have been less rigid. In this way, the contemporary interpretation of the Constitution profoundly affects the style of the control of dangerous substances—in accordance, it should be added, with reputable medical opinion and popular attitudes toward drug use.

Public Fear

Examination of the health professions at the time when the fundamental drug control laws were enacted also brings an understanding of the motivation for and the form of the laws enacted. In the evolution of drug laws, the American medical profession, as it formally interacted with the government and the community, is shown to have been profoundly affected by the currents of public fear and concerns. One can conclude from the history of the medical profession's contribution to the various laws that a greater effort should be made to separate what is actually demonstrated in clinical research and the social implications of that research as interpreted by medical spokesmen. The danger to public policy formation arises from the appearance of scientific objectivity that may be given to what is actually a strongly felt social or political judgment. The medical and legal professions have often been as persuaded of the truth or significance of inaccurate and passionate judgments as everyone else.

To take a few examples, Dr. Williams, quoted previously on the effects of cocaine on southern blacks, was repeating a belief that was widespread before World War I. Yet, there is evidence from the records of state mental hospitals and from the practice of

9. Comprehensive Drug Abuse Prevention and Control Act of 1970, 84 Stat. 1236 (codified in scattered sections of 21, 42 U.S.C.).

southern narcotic clinics that the baneful effect of cocaine on blacks was neither particularly common nor the direct cause of violence. However, in the popular sentiment of the times, cocaine was associated with black hostility and, thus, was said to contribute indirectly to massive repression of black voting and other civil rights around the turn of the century. Cocaine became a convenient explanation for violent crimes or even open hostility by blacks; it became a convenient explanation for racial and social tensions. This symbolic use of cocaine permitted a simple formula for social harmony. If cocaine were eliminated—and perhaps alcohol as well—you would have a docile and cooperative black population. The attractiveness of such an explanation for trouble with a restless and exploited group is obvious—blame is placed on an inert substance rather than on complex and emotional factors.

In its first encounter with American society, heroin prompted, in part, not ethnic tension but, rather, fear of a stage of life—adolescence. During and after World War I, heroin characterized threats from—to use a favored expression of the times—"youthful debauchees," or rebellious adolescents. It also served as a popular cause for the crime wave which was widely claimed to have spread over the nation after World War I. For example, in 1925 the New York City Commissioner of Correction warned:

> Heroin . . . is the most insidious and crime-inspiring of all drugs. When we consider that the United States uses more of the powerful opiates than all the leading nations of Europe combined we begin to understand why there are more murders in a single American city than in all the countries of Western Europe. In my opinion, no measure is too radical or severe that would prohibit the manufacture and sale of habit-forming drugs.

By such descriptions and beliefs, the drug became linked with cocaine's euphoric and stimulating effects. Thus, the AMA spokesman before Congress related what would be a logical deduction from the popular image and explanation for heroin use, but still he did not accurately describe its physiological effects which were known to research physicians in 1924. One gets the impression that the prohibition of heroin was thought to be so important to the public welfare that the medical profession should, out of public spirit, support the movement without quibbling over the pharmacological effects of the drug. Dr. Lawrence Kolb, Sr., who was then the Public Health Service's narcotics expert, tried to explain that heroin and morphine were essentially the same and did not physiologically stimulate violence. He said there was more violence in a gallon of alcohol than in a ton of opium. But no one was interested. Therefore, we can conclude that it is likely that a drug, if identified with a group that is the source of social fear, will have attributed to it the dangers said to come from the group; consequently, the drug cannot be accurately evaluated in the political process once it becomes an essential part of a common-sense explanation for a social problem. In such a situation, one might expect the influential medical profession to inject reality into the controversy, but too often the profession, as well as everyone else, is caught up in the belief.

There is another observation worth noting. Medical and legal objections, such as those made by Dr. Kolb, to extravagant descriptions of heroin were simply ignored if other professionals testified in accordance with public fears. The fears of the public helped determine what was valid medical testimony. Only the most vigorous professional protest has had much chance of deflecting public pressure from simplistic and punitive solutions to complex social problems. And, of course, the power and threat of an aroused public is a warning to professional leaders—opposition to a popular explanation for social disorder can be politically unwise, or even fatal.

The linking of a drug to a social threat can be caused by growing racial or generational tension; it can be further inculcated through determined and sustained propaganda campaigns. Such campaigns often reiterate and exaggerate popular impressions of drug dangers. Consider one of the most successful national campaigns—that conducted in the 1920s and into the 1930s by Admiral Richmond Pearson Hobson, a hero of the Spanish-American War and a former congressman. He was a vigorous proponent of Prohibition and an eloquent platform speaker. There is no question that Admiral Hobson was sincere in his attempt to arouse America to the dangers of heroin and marihuana, but the overly fearful descriptions he employed, and his wide acceptance in some of the most respected elements of society, meant that the message he gave was harmful. For example, he considered heroin a direct stimulus to senseless violence and preached that one dose of heroin, even if unwittingly eaten in an adulterated ice cream cone, would be addicting. Hobson established national and international organizations to wage the campaign against heroin. During the 1920s he mobilized the radio, service clubs, congressional clout, educators, magazines, etc., to give an exaggerated and distorted vision of heroin's dangers. In the early 1930s he switched his primary concern to marihuana and faithfully spread blood-curdling horror stories about cannabis. Always, he believed that the best way to fight drug use was through propaganda campaigns which painted drugs as the ultimate in evil and degeneration.

Enactment of the Marihuana Tax Act of 1937 [10] provides another example of the ways in which a drug came to be associated with an increasingly feared and repressed ethnic group. The Agriculture Department in 1920 had published a pamphlet urging Americans to grow cannabis as a profitable undertaking. The pamphlet provided, for example, all rules for planting marihuana. Yet, as the 1920s progressed, immigrants from Mexico poured into the nation at the request of agricultural growers to harvest beets and other farm products; tensions mounted in those communities where the Chicanos gathered. The custom of some Chicanos of growing and smoking cannabis ultimately was identified with troubles between Anglos and Chicanos. Former Narcotics Commis-

10. Act of Aug. 2, 1937, ch. 553, 50 Stat. 551.

sioner Harry Anslinger recalls that the pressure for a federal anti-marihuana law came from the areas of the nation in which Chicanos were considered a threat to the Anglo communities—that is, the American Southwest.

Supported by a combination of fearful medical opinion, ethnic tensions, and political pressure, the Marihuana Tax Act was passed.[11]   But it wasn't easy to outlaw a weed. Therefore—and here is another example of legal ingenuity comparable to the Supreme Court's outlawing of addiction maintenance—the Roosevelt administration proposed a law controlling marihuana. The administration did that, not by formally prohibiting it (which would have been unconstitutional), but by making it, like machine guns, subject to a transfer tax. Here again, the common opinion of the medical profession and the ingenuity of the legal profession collaborated to provide what appeared to be a public necessity: the reassurance that there was a national defense to a supposed drug danger. Marihuana became linked with Chicanos as smoking opium had been identified with the Chinese, cocaine with southern blacks, and heroin with young criminals. Each social tension or prejudice could be explained by a drug, and vice versa. The result was, for all practical effects, total prohibition with extreme punitive measures. The regrettable result of explaining social disorder and tension directly and simply by the use of a particular substance is that anger, fear, and frustration make unlikely both flexible regulation and reasonable punishments for use and sale. The punishments may become so severe that the probability of injustice to some poorly defended individual rises and the probability of consistent deterrence decreases.

Lessons from History

There is, of course, no perfect way for society to work. Mistakes are inevitable and justice is never swift or sure enough.

---

11. *Ibid.*

But by examining and understanding the past, we can at least ask if the temptation to eliminate evildoers by horrendous punishments represents an accurate estimate of what is best for society in the short or long term, or if it is simply an expression of frustration.

Chapter 4

Studies

The final report of the National Commission on Marihuana and Drug Abuse examines and questions the validity of several assumptions, such as: (1) that there is a distinction between hard and soft drugs; (2) that the easiest way to deal with the drug problem is to eliminate the source of the drug; (3) that in regard to treatment and rehabilitation, people want to be helped; and (4) that if you give people information, they will react to it in a rational manner.

The commission report, which has been both condemned and applauded, deals with such controversial subjects as methadone maintenance, control, prohibition, terminology, the British experience, and education. It has been called the most comprehensive report ever made in the United States on this topic. But in spite of its national significance, the report and its 110 recommendations were almost totally ignored by the media, and received a poor reception at the White House as well. Regardless of response, however, the existence of the report testifies to the seriousness of the drug problem and the recognition that it simply will not go away through inattention.

The Authors

Michael R. Sonnenreich
Drug Abuse: A National Report

Mr. Sonnenreich serves as executive director of the National Commission on Marihuana and Drug Abuse, which was established by Congress in 1970 to conduct a comprehensive study and investigation of the causes of the drug problem. A graduate of Harvard Law School, he previously served as deputy general counsel to the Bureau of Narcotics and Dangerous Drugs.

James Markham
Legal and Medical Approaches to the Drug Problem

Mr. Markham has been a staff reporter for the *New York Times* since 1971, specializing in problems of drug abuse. He is a 1965 graduate of Princeton University and was a Rhodes Scholar at Balliol College, Oxford University from 1965-1967. He served as a correspondent for the Associated Press in South Asia and West Africa from 1967-1971.

Jonathan Leff
Licit and Illicit Drugs

Mr. Leff has been a staff member for ten years at Consumers Union of United States, Inc., the organization that evaluates consumer goods and services. As director of special publications, he is concerned mainly with the books and booklets published by Consumers Union, and was directly involved with the preparation of *Licit and Illicit Drugs*. Mr. Leff has also worked as an editor and writer in commercial book, magazine, and newspaper publishing, and in public relations.

Sander Vanocur
Where the Media Fails

Mr. Vanocur, veteran broadcast journalist, served on the staff of the *Manchester Guardian* and did commentary for the BBC. He was a reporter for the *New York Times* before joining NBC in 1957, and was a correspondent for NBC until 1971 when he resigned to become senior correspondent for National Public Affairs Center for television, the public affairs programming center for public television. Mr. Vanocur is presently consultant to the Center for the Study of Democratic Institutions in California.

Robert Hughes
The Power of Suggestion
Mr. Hughes is chief of Metromedia Radio's Washington News Bureau and
news director of WASH-FM, the Metromedia Station serving the nation's
capitol. Before that he had served as news editor, newscaster, and correspondent with Metromedia. Mr. Hughes won the Associated Press Award for
outstanding in-depth reporting in 1972 for the documentary "Magic in the
Music," a study of the FCC's controversial order on "drug lyrics" in popular
music.

Drug Abuse:
A National Report

MICHAEL R. SONNENREICH
The final report of the National
Commission on Marihuana and Drug Abuse has been called the
most comprehensive report ever made in the United States on this
topic. The most important thing that you should recognize about
commission reports in general is that they are usually ahead of
their time. Because commissions do not have the bureaucratic bias,
they generally make statements that do not have general appli-
cability for three to five years. However, the report officially
exists, and you can agree or disagree with it as a matter of conscience.

Problems inevitably arise in this country when we are told
that we have a problem. For instance, we have not been told that
we have an alcohol problem, so we do not worry about it. But we
have been told that we have a drug problem, so we *do* worry about
drug abuse.

About four years ago we spent a total of some $66.4 million
for the entire federal effort in the drug abuse area, including law
enforcement, treatment, prevention, and education. That is the

equivalent, for those who like to make comparisons, of approximately three and one-half F-14 fighter planes for the Navy. Estimates are that we will have exceeded the $1 billion mark in 1973. When we reach that point, we become—for want of a better term—a drug-abuse industrial complex.

Terminology

Real dilemmas become manifest when we start to look at this problem. We have had rapid funding with very little questioning of either basic assumptions or the definitions that explain what we are talking about. Words like "addiction" and "narcotics" and "drug abuse" are thrown around. These are terms which, over the years, have absolutely lost their meaning and have become social code words. They are not medical words. We really do not have a workable vocabulary in this area, especially since the words are used to connote nothing more than social disapproval. In fact, the term "drug abuse" now simply means something of which we socially disapprove. It is a term that fluctuates in harmony with the mores of society. Those who lived in the Mediterranean area around 1600 and smoked tobacco had their heads chopped off—their crime was drug abuse.

We have circumscribed those drugs which we consider unacceptable for use. The commission is asking, among other things, whether we drew our circle correctly. Are there other drugs that belong within the circle? Are there drugs that go without the circle, such as alcohol and tobacco? Why did we draw the circle the way we did?

One of the reasons that we drew the circle this way is because some drugs simply have been culturally accepted and others have not. Some are indigenous to the United States and others are not. Tobacco and alcohol have been with us for a long time. Sir Walter Raleigh is legendary. Alexis de Tocqueville wrote of the propensity of the American public to consume spirits over 100 years ago.

The problem is, though, that we keep *talking* about drugs. Until about the early 1900s that was fine, because there were not too many drugs to worry about. However, with the growth and development of pharmacology and new drugs, the old terms lost meaning; unfortunately, instead of disappearing from the vernacular, they changed into social words. Consequently, the commission wanted to eliminate words like "addiction" and "narcotics" and "drug abuse"—words that cannot describe the problem we are looking at—and asked whether we were really looking at drugs.

The Commission

The commission felt we were not really looking at drugs. The things that are important from our point of view as policy makers, not as lawyers or doctors, are the social risks and the social costs. If there are only minimal social costs due to some activity, or if the public risks are small, then, as policy makers, we have to ask ourselves whether we want to do anything about that activity.

We do not want to become involved with private health concerns. For example, we are not terribly interested in learning if your lung falls down to your kneecap as a result of smoking cigarettes. That is your problem, and the problem of your doctor, hospital, and insurance company. Those concerns are not determinative when deciding whether to use the government. Under our system, there must be a justifiable reason for the government to become involved.

Hard vs. Soft Drugs

The first assumption that was critically examined in preparing the report was that there is a distinction to be made between a hard drug and a soft drug. Everyone has heard that heroin and the opiates are hard drugs, the usual explanation being that they are physically addictive. But is physical addiction the major concern, and is it the one that escalates drug concern to the government?

One of the commissioners is Dr. Maurice H. Seevers, chairman of the Department of Pharmacology at the University of Michigan. Dr. Seevers is in charge of the monkey colony for the United States government. For forty years now, all psychoactive drugs that we have discovered or uncovered have been sent to Dr. Seevers, and he tests them on his monkeys. He has approximately 450 monkeys, some dogs, some cats, and one parrot. (We have never determined why he has the parrot.)

We put the monkeys in cages; we put catheter tubes down into their stomachs; and we give them a little light and a bar to press. We teach the monkey to hit the bar, and every time he hits the bar, he gets a drug. If the monkey likes the drug, he hits the bar many times. This is recorded on a computer. We let them have a good time for about two weeks; in other words, we give them free access to the drugs to see what kind of drug reinforcement there is and to plot their tolerance curve. After two weeks we take away the drug. The monkey goes over and he hits the bar—nothing; he hits the bar again—nothing. After a while, the monkey gives up.

The machine records up to 6,400 bar presses a day. With the physically dependent opiate drugs, the bar is pressed an average of 162 times a day before the monkey gives up. When dealing with the amphetamines, which are not physically addictive, the monkey bar is pressed an average of 1,800 times a day. With cocaine, which is not physically addicting, the monkey presses an average of 6,400 times a day.

Therefore, the old assumption that hard drugs are more deadly than soft drugs really means little. One thing we did discover with the monkeys using cocaine—and this is one of the reasons we are very concerned about this drug—is that, given free access, the monkeys will press the bar until they die. There are only two known drugs for which the monkeys will not press a second time unless forced—LSD and mescaline. They will press for other hallucinogenic drugs but not for those two, so perhaps they know something that we do not.

This assumption differentiating between hard and soft drugs is really subject to very serious questioning and raises the point of whether we should be concentrating on the drugs. Do we care what the drug is, or do we really care about the behavior that results from the drug's use? The commission's feeling is that we should be concerned with the consequences of use.

Drug Source

Another assumption that was examined was that the easiest way to deal with the problem is to eliminate the source of the drug. This is a very legitimate initial concern, because if you are trying to eliminate drugs, it should be done across the whole spectrum of concern. However, to think that you can eliminate drugs that are growing wild, such as coca leaf, opium, poppy, and cannabis, does not seem realistic. There is no question that we should do something about eliminating the source, but it must be a long-range strategy. In addition, restricting availability is only a part of the problem, because if the demand continues, someone is going to discover a way to synthesize drugs that have nearly the same effects.

Treatment

With respect to treatment and rehabilitation, there is an implicit assumption that people want to be helped. The commission has some serious questions as to whether that is true across the entire spectrum of persons who are heroin dependent. Many persons do not want to be helped and simply drop out of society as a means of escape. They drop out to alcohol; they drop out to heroin. One sees much cross-tolerance and cross-substitution between the two. The question centers upon the degree to which people want to drop out and their relative desire to get involved with what is commonly referred to as the "hustle." We may have to begin testing our approach to treatment and rehabilitation, because it may not be true that everyone wants to have a job, raise a family, and cope with all the problems of middle class life.

Education

We also tested our assumptions about education. The assumption was that if you give people information they will react in a rational manner to it. Experience has indicated otherwise. The education programs in the United States are presently somewhat haphazard because they have never been systematically evaluated. We are not certain whether the information dispersed is turning people off or on. It is a very difficult thing to analyze because it is only one factor among many variables. Yet, we have pigeonholed the problem and now we are assuming that there is some way to deal with it. The commission has recommended a moratorium on these education programs until there has been some sort of rational analysis. Why spend the money if we do not know what the real results are? Remember that this drug-abuse industrial complex is a business—a very real business. When $1 billion is spent at the federal level, and probably three times that amount at the state level, you are in big business. There is a tendency for bureaucracies to follow Newton's Law of Physics, i.e., that a body in motion tends to stay in motion. It is very difficult to stop a bureaucracy that is building momentum.

Institutionalizing Drug Problems

There is a tendency to institutionalize problems and one of the commission's concerns is that we may be institutionalizing the drug problem as a continuing part of the American way of life. There is a premium placed on describing any problem in ever more and more grotesque terms because that will generate ever more and more federal spending.

It becomes a sort of chicken-egg situation with the end result that, in many instances, the system awards failure rather than success. If you take the entire heroin-dependent population of a city, work with them, treat them, and cure them, then you do not get funded the following year. Hence, the tendency to institutionalize the program to be assured of federal funding.

We are not as interested in drugs per se as we are in breaking the circle. Alcohol is doubtless part of the circle. There is a certain hypocrisy to speak of alcohol as food, or of tobacco as a cash crop—so dubbed by the Department of Agriculture—and of all the other drugs as drugs. Therefore, it is best to begin analyzing this problem in terms of consequences rather than nomenclature.

When we talk about the social costs, we must consider both sides of the equation. We are worried about acute effects at the compulsive end of the scale—the drug-dependent person—because of the other factors involved, but we must also be concerned with the social costs of the institutional response to the problem. There are costs involved in instituting responses, whether they be methadone maintenance programs, law enforcement programs, or baggage inspection at customs. These things must be weighed in the balance. You must recognize that there is a cost to each institutional response. Some of the costs of response may deal with the very cost of the problem identified. For example, the rate of crime certainly reflects property crimes committed by drug-dependent persons. However, just because you recognize that one institutional response may cause persons to commit crimes because they cannot buy a drug legally does not automatically condemn the response. Other factors must be weighed.

When we decide to treat heroin-dependent individuals, we spend not only money, but we deplete a most important resource—the human beings in the medical and social work fields. That is a finite resource, and when they are placed in the drug-dependence area, they are taken away from some other important area. This factor must be weighted in the equation to determine whether the response should be that great. Perhaps we should have only ten persons instead of twenty, and put ten in mental retardation or ten in cancer, and things like that. It certainly is a subjective judgment—but it is one that must be made.

Drug Use

Drug use is not unique; it is symptomatic of a range of other things. The casual relationships are few. Individuals use drugs for a variety of reasons, reasons which stem from other causes, such as boredom or poverty. It is easy to talk about getting someone off heroin; the more important thing is restructuring him back into society, if he wants to come back. The question should be asked whether we want to eliminate drug use; it is likely that we will always have some degree of it. Also, when people say they want to eliminate drug use, they are not including alcohol and tobacco. Rather than eliminate it, we want to restructure drug use so that it is *responsible* use. There are always going to be persons who will use drugs, no matter how concerned we are about it. The goal is to keep this down to an irreducible minimum. That has been the response of the federal government and the states.

The ideal may be nice, but reality is in direct conflict with it. For some strange reason, in every society man has ever formed, he has managed to find the one thing that can turn him on—be it alcohol or a mushroom—and he has structured its use. But the point is that man does find it, and we have to accept that.

If you were told today that unemployment in the United States is four per cent, everyone would feel relieved, because you have been told that four per cent is a rate that indicates as many people are employed as want to be. We would accept four per cent. If you were told that unemployment was ten per cent, you would get very nervous and start hoarding your money. Perhaps we should be thinking about drug use and other social concerns in very much the same fashion. There is some percentage of our population that will become drug dependent; the issue is whether this is a percentage of the population we can carry. Perhaps we should start looking at the problem in terms of cost-benefit and restructure our responses. We are carrying ten million alcoholics right now.

We have been concerned about all institutional responses dealing with the drug problem as a drug monolith. We do not talk about marihuana or heroin except when we want to have arguments; we talk about the drug problem. It is a code word used because we really do not look behind that drug monolith. What the commission tried to do, since we were interested in behavior, was to find out what kind of behavior we were talking about. We divided it down into several gross categories, and focused upon motivation and frequency of use.

The largest of such categories of drug use is experimental use. This is not an unusual kind of behavior; in fact, we tell our youth to experiment and to be inquisitive. Most of us took some alcohol before the legal age; some of us smoked cigarettes; this was part of growing up. Youth today also experiment with the forbidden, including drugs. This must be recognized in our institutional approach. It is highly unlikely that we will halt experimentation by our youth, and hence the response should be tailored toward trying to move that kind of curiosity and experimentation into more acceptable social channels.

The second area, social recreational use, is also widespread. People decide that they are going to use drugs, including alcohol, for social purposes. We all go to cocktail parties. If one were to ask what drugs have social recreational use in the United States today, the response would be alcohol, tobacco, and marihuana. But in comparison to marihuana, alcohol is used much more frequently. The patterns of marihuana use in the United States simply do not approach those of alcohol. The statistics also indicate that marihuana will not replace alcohol.

Those who have just left college are using alcohol more and using marihuana less. They have discovered alcohol as a great new drug. Our surveys showed that forty-five per cent of our youth and fifty per cent of the adults who have used marihuana have used it in combination with alcohol, probably Boone's Farm apple wine. You can categorize marihuana as a recreational drug because, according to our national survey, at least twenty-six million Americans have used it at least once, and thirteen million categorize themselves as present users.

We also note that marihuana use is very age-specific. The heaviest use is between the ages of eighteen and twenty-one and it decreases sharply at about age twenty-five. The saturation point is at the college level—69.9 per cent of those in college have used marihuana. However, use is intermittent—less than once a month. It is not the kind of social lubricant that alcohol is, and there is serious doubt, given our cultural background, that it ever will be.

The third category is very perplexing; we call it circumstantial or situational drug use. Fundamentally, it is displayed by the athlete who takes his amphetamines or steroids to perform better and the truck driver who takes his amphetamines to stay alert. Drug use was very clearly situational in Vietnam—easy availability of a cheap drug, combined with the boredom and fright of the most vulnerable age group, led to heavy use. Yet, studies indicate that no more than ten per cent of the soldiers there had ever used heroin and that there was a very high drop-off when they came back to the United States. Over ninety per cent never went back to heroin.

The fourth category is intensified use, best characterized by the social drinker, the happy housewife in suburbia who pops her barbiturates, and the executive who has graduated from Digel to Librium. This is not a total lifestyle, but it becomes a large part of the lifestyle. Drugs are used to cope with stress and anxiety. That use represents the beginning of drug dependence.

Obviously, the last category is compulsive drug use, which is best characterized by the skid row alcoholic or the heroin-dependent person.

Legal Approaches

This country has dealt with drugs under three different legal approaches. We operate on a punitive premise, a therapeutic premise, and a preventive premise.

The punitive premise is very clear; you are told not to do something, you exercise your free choice and do it, and you are punished. Despite all the euphemisms you can think of, we punish you whether you like it or not because it is part of our nature. The punitive premise has been applied in the drug area, and as long as one can control the user's actions, there is some legal validity to that premise.

There is another premise called the therapeutic approach, which combines the legal and medical professions. In 1962 the Supreme Court said in *Robinson* v. *California*[12] that heroin dependence (they said addiction) is an illness, and this gave impetus to the rise of the therapeutic premise which is paternalistic. This civil commitment has always been treated as a diversion from the criminal justice system, and we are concerned because this civil paternalistic approach has not been adequately safeguarded. If the therapeutic premise is to cure people, they can be kept under treatment forever, because it may be impossible to cure them of heroin dependence. We must consider the rights of those who are in treatment programs.

The Supreme Court evidenced its concern in 1972 in *Jackson* v. *Indiana*[13] when it wondered why anyone was challenging the civil commitment laws. We presently have 194,000 people in federal, state, and local jails, and we have 428,000 people committed to mental institutions. The main question concerns the

12. Robinson v. California, 370 U.S. 660 (1962).
13. 406 U.S. 715 (1972).

rights of those people, and I think both the lawyers and the doctors in this group will become involved in this important area.

The last area is the preventive premise about which you hear so much. It generally takes the phraseology, "Let's sweep the streets clean, pick them up, put them on an island, and float it out into the Pacific." The preventive premise makes great sense when you talk about communicable diseases like bubonic plague and smallpox. We recognize that no one chooses to get bubonic plague; therefore, if someone comes to this country with bubonic plague, the law can reach out, grab him, and quarantine him.

But do not be fooled with medical terms when speaking of drugs. You hear the words "epidemic" and "contagion." It is a contagion, but not a medical contagion. The transmission of drugs is not by bacteria and microbes; it is by thought. We cannot prevent the communication of ideas. We may not like the ideas; we may want to alter the message so that we do not have a spread in drug use, but the point is that we do not exercise a legal premise to implement such a change. Do not get caught up in words without examining them. We are not talking about a medical disease, but first about amendment issues—the communication of ideas. We should spend money and devote effort, but we should not forget the larger social issues involved.

Legal and Medical Approaches to the Drug Problem

JAMES MARKHAM   The beauty of this report of the National Commission on Marihuana and Drug Abuse is that it keeps alive a necessary tension between two approaches to addiction that have been dominant at various times and in various places and quarters in this country. One is the medical approach which assumes that if you can do something about the man's drug problem—remove the drug from him—you have cured his problems and society's related problems. The opposite is the criminal approach which is a combination of what one would call punitive and interventionist approaches. This has been the culturally dominant approach throughout this century and is still the most attractive one in political circles. Governor Rockefeller's recent wisdom in locking up violent addicts is typical of this approach and may represent the drift of the political-public, unenlightened sector of our nation. Fortunately, however, a significant number of persons are now tending to drift toward the medical model. This is apotheosized in one sense by the Consumers Union; the Consumers Union report embodies the most intelligent form, but it, too, is subject to fault when it criticizes the medical approach.

The danger is that we approach this drug problem bristling a bit. Liberals, as "right-thinking people," tend to have negative preconceptions about the criminal model. We are repulsed by the proponents and by the essential reprehensibleness of the criminal approach. Hence, we lurch left into the medical solution, which, again, in its simplest form is maintenance—if you cannot remove the drug from the user, give it to him and let him be.

We have to get beyond the drugs to the persons who use them and the reasons why they do. We should not let the drugs themselves obfuscate how we react to the problem.

Drug Abuse Report

In certain quarters of this country (like Charles River), there will be persons who will find the marihuana report a timid document. This group will doubtless believe that the commission lacked the courage to go the whole way and propose abolishing the crime of possession. The commission wrestled with anguish. If you read the pertinent section, you will see that it is partially a copout. The commission came to the conclusion that possession laws have no real functional utility, but, rather, have a kind of symbolic value—society does not want to legitimize the possession of heroin. That is a decision that society can indeed make. The commission, however, made a different decision about marihuana. Yet, there will still be individuals who think the report is a copout. Others will believe that the commission was not afraid of public indignation, but, rather, made an intelligent decision to retain the tension between the medical and criminal approaches.

Solutions

The junkie in America belongs neither to the American Bar Association (ABA) nor to the American Medical Association (AMA). He is somewhere in between. Lawyers especially love to seize on the medical model since it is so beautifully logical. The addict's problem is his drug. Give him the drug and you are finished with the problem. But it may be—and this is especially true in heroin addiction—that the problems the man brought to drug-taking have a lot more to do with the behavior to which we so object.

Neither of the professions have performed in a totally admirable manner in this area. They have been making the same mistakes as the general population. If you keep alive in yourself that unwillingness to have certainty in this field thrust upon you either as oppression or benign, paternalistic compassion—this poor man is taking drugs—if you can remain skeptical of both of those poles, that will be a contribution.

Licit and Illicit Drugs

JONATHAN LEFF

In comparing the report of the National Commission on Marihuana and Drug Abuse with the Consumers

Union's report, *Licit and Illicit Drugs,* the commission shares a good deal of the union's philosophy, but there are differences in certain very important areas.

Prohibition

The commission report states that the use of illicit drugs, particularly marihuana, increased dramatically during the 1960s in spite of draconian penalties. This occurred at least in part because of the draconian penalties and the accompanying policies that followed. We believe that prohibition does not work—alcohol prohibition did not work and, as the country has been learning since 1914, the time of the Harrison Act,[14] heroin prohibition does not work either. Prohibition simply raises prices, thus attracting more entrepreneurs to the drug market. If the drug is addicting and the price escalation is carried to outrageous extremes, as in the case of heroin, addicts resort to crime to finance their purchases at a tragic cost, not only in dollars, but in community disruption and personal destruction. Prohibition also transforms the market from relatively bland substances to more hazardous concentrates which are more readily smuggled and marketed—from opium smoking to heroin mainlining, from coca leaves to cocaine, and from marihuana to hashish. Prohibition opens the door to adulterated and contaminated drugs. Worst of all, excessive reliance on prohibition laws and enforcement lulls the country, decade after decade, into a false confidence that nothing more needs to be done except to pass yet another law, to hire a few hundred more narcotics agents, or to give license to break down doors without knocking first.

Drug Use

One of the most significant contributions of the commission report is the data on percentage change in student use of drugs

14. Act of Dec. 17, 1914, ch. 1, § 1, 38 Stat. 785.

from 1969 to 1972. During that period of concentrated effort by the federal government in the drug field, the report indicates that, among young people who tried various types of drugs at least once, opiate use rose 218 per cent among junior high school students, 5 per cent among senior high school students, and 18 per cent among college students. The use of LSD and other hallucinogens rose 50 per cent among junior high school students, 133 per cent among senior high school students, and 133 per cent among college students. The use of marihuana rose 60 per cent among junior high school students, and so on. This is a shocking testament to the efficacy of the present system.

Terminology

The commission report makes much of the ostensible need to discard certain terms, including the word "addiction." In its place, the report turns to the terms "heroin dependent" and "compulsive use" and "drug dependent" and, occasionally, "severe dependence." Later, in at least two places, "drug dependence" is categorized as an illness of the spirit for which the commission says, "As in the case of other social maladjustments, there are no quick solutions." We find little but confusion to be gained by such euphemisms or by such mysticisms; we have found the terms "addicting" and "addiction" to be precise, adequate, and useful.

Addiction

There are three basic attributes to an addicting drug: physical dependence with a withdrawal syndrome when the drug is abruptly discontinued; tolerance so that the effects gradually disappear if the same dose is taken repeatedly; and craving during abstinence with a tendency to resume drug-seeking behavior. That last, the matter of craving, does not appear to have impressed the commission very much. Yet, it is well known that long after withdrawal the addict will experience, from time to time, waves of anxiety, depression, and craving. The response ultimately, except in very, very few cases, is to return to the drug. Mr. Sonnenreich said that "getting someone off heroin is no great feat." One might add that *keeping* him off is the problem.

Heroin

Whatever the cause of addiction—psychological, sociological, or biochemical—we believe this about heroin as an addicting drug. The following is taken from *Licit and Illicit Drugs:*

> The time has come to recognize what should have been obvious since 1914—that heroin is a drug most users go right on using despite the threat of imprisonment, despite actual imprisonment for years, despite repeated "cures" and long-time residence in rehabilitation centers, and despite the risk of disease and even death. Heroin is a drug for which addicts will prostitute themselves. It is also a drug to which most addicts return despite a sincere desire to "stay clean," a resolve to stay clean, and even . . . success (sometimes enforced by confinement) in staying clean for weeks, months, or years. This is what is meant by the statement that heroin is an addicting drug.
>
> . . . Almost all heroin addicts, it is true, do stop taking heroin from time to time. But almost all subsequently relapse. . . . By publicizing the few conspicuous exceptions, the handful of successful ex-heroin addicts, and by assuming that others can readily follow in their foot-steps, harm is done in at least three tragic ways:
>
> (1) Another generation of young people is persuaded that heroin addiction is temporary. They are falsely assured that the worst that can happen to them if they get hooked on heroin is that they may have to spend a year or two in a drug treatment center, or, better yet, in a therapeutic community, after which they will emerge, heads high, as certified ex-addicts.
>
> (2) Hundreds of millions of dollars are wasted on vast . . . "treatment programs" that almost totally fail to curb subsequent heroin use by addicts, while more pressing methods are skimped on.

(3) Law enforcement resources are wasted on futile efforts to keep heroin away from heroin addicts instead of concentrating on the essential task: . . . keeping heroin away from nonaddicts.

There is one major exception to the rule that most heroin addicts go right on using heroin or return to heroin. The heroin addict can comfortably do without his drug if supplied with a related drug, such as methadone. Unlike heroin, it can be effectively taken orally rather than by injection. One of its other advantages is that it need be taken only once a day instead of several times. Like heroin, it has very little effect on either mind or body if taken regularly. Most important, methadone is legal and it is cheap.

Maintenance

The commission supports methadone maintenance as "the most significant form of drug treatment available," but in its understandable concern for the methadone patient, the commission fails to recognize an equally important potential for methadone maintenance—the sharp curtailment of the heroin black-market. Methadone is not a panacea, but since it is legal and cheap, it can free the heroin addict from his life of crime and from the other disastrous consequences of the heroin black-market.

The heroin black-market must be abolished and the only way it can be abolished is by eliminating the demands for black-market heroin. Contrary to the commission, the union believes that methadone maintenance can and does make a significant reduction in drug-related crime.

On the central issue of narcotic addiction, accordingly, Consumers Union recommends: (1) that the United States' policies and practices be promptly revised to ensure that no narcotics addict need get his drug from the black-market; (2) that methadone maintenance be promptly made available under medical auspices to every narcotics addict who applies for it; and (3) that other forms of narcotic maintenance, including opium, morphine, and heroin maintenance, be made available along with methadone maintenance under medical auspices on a carefully planned experimental basis.

The third of these recommendations—that experimental opium, morphine, and heroin, as well as methadone, be made available to addicts—is based, in part, on the unassailable fact that an addict is personally far better off on legal, low-cost, medicinally pure narcotics than he is on exorbitantly priced, dangerously adulterated and contaminated black-market heroin. Similarly, society is better off when addicts receive their drugs legally at low cost or free of charge.

The union's recommendation for experimental opium, morphine, and heroin maintenance programs is not based on any confidence that they will prove superior to maintenance on methadone. All of the data so far indicate that methadone is very nearly the ideal maintenance drug. The ready availability of an excellent maintenance drug—and there are some 85,000 narcotics addicts on methadone maintenance in the United States today—is not a sound reason, however, for abandoning the search for an even better one. Even if in the end the trials of opium, morphine, and heroin maintenance merely buttress the conclusion that methadone is the drug of choice, the research will have served a useful purpose since oral methadone has so far only proved its worth in competition with black-market heroin. The next challenge oral methadone should be required to meet is a carefully controlled comparison with legal opium, morphine, and heroin, injectable methadone, and perhaps with other drugs. The tests should be designed to determine, once and for all, whether the heroin molecule itself or the mystique surrounding it makes the difference.

British Experience

We should examine the British experience with narcotics. Great Britain and the United States began with essentially the same base a century ago when opiates were generally available. Through the years the two countries' problems were essentially the same until the United States turned in the direction of the Harrison Act [15] and the repression that followed. The British continued treating narcotic addiction as a medical problem. Indeed, in the early 1920s they sent Dr. Harry Campbell here to study American methods. He returned to England aghast, saying, in effect: My God, they treat their narcotics addicts as criminals over there. Let's keep our present system.

Our understanding of the British experience does not square with that which appears in the commission report. One statement made is that in 1968, after a significant increase in the number of drug-dependent persons in Great Britain, the British practice changed. It is our understanding that the increase actually followed the institution of closer renotification of addicts and reflected understandable duplication. In the years that followed, the number dropped significantly. The report also states that a system was created which permits maintenance doses to be distributed only through government-authorized clinics. It is our understanding that if you want heroin, you must go to a clinic, but that if you are willing to accept methadone, you can get it from a physician. This reflects an effort by the British government to turn the narcotics addict in Great Britain toward methadone.

As of the end of 1971, there were approximately 1,555 narcotics addicts registered with the Home Office in the United Kingdom. According to the head of the Home Office, there are very few additional hidden addicts, those who deal solely in the black-market. There are a few square blocks of New York City where you can find 2,000 addicts.

The commission report suggests that a significant reason for the British success, and our inability to adopt their approach, is that the British population really is not like ours. At the same time, however, the report makes an occasional reference to the

15. *Ibid.*

success of certain approaches of the Japanese. But the Japanese population is not like ours either.

Nicotine

The union does not agree with the commission's decision on nicotine. The report states: "The word 'addict' was commonly used to describe the tobacco habit despite the absence of significant drug-abuse behavior arising from its use." There are similar references to the fact that nicotine is not an addicting drug, not a drug-dependent drug as the commission describes it. In *Licit and Illicit Drugs,* tobacco is described as one of the most physiologically damaging substances used by man: "Since nicotine is one of the most perniciously addicting drugs in common use, most tobacco users are hooked and, in effect, locked to the damaging effects of tobacco." Doctor M. A. H. Russell of the Addiction Research Unit of the Institute of Psychiatry in London, which now has added nicotine addiction to its studies, put it this way: "If it were not for the nicotine in tobacco smoke, people would be little more inclined to smoke cigarettes than they are to blow bubbles or light sparklers."

Where the Media Fails

SANDER VANOCUR
The chief virtue of the report of the National Commission on Marihuana and Drug Abuse is its modesty. Kenneth Galbraith says that modesty is a highly overrated virtue. But to someone who has been trying to wander around in this darkness for a few years, always learning more and less at the same time, the document is useful for saying how little we know

about the problem. One of the great problems we have in this society is knowing really so little. How so many of our leaders can act with such certainty about the drug problem with such little knowledge is amazing.

The Media

One of the chief problems is the media. Following the release of the report, NBC did a fairly credible job—they interviewed Ray Shafer and Ron Nessen and indicated that President Nixon was not very happy about the report. CBS, which in recent months has been doing these things much better than any other network, had about twenty-five seconds of copy by Roger Mudd. Apparently neither the major networks nor PBS had a special report on that night. You may ask if Nelson Rockefeller is making proposals, if President Nixon is urging a more punitive approach, if this is one of our major problems that people, rightly or wrongly, associate as being connected with crime, then do not the newspapers and the television news departments of this country have some kind of responsibility to indulge in other than the shorthand they usually use to describe this problem?

Around May of 1970, the New York papers were attacking the methadone experiment, which Dr. Dole was just developing. The code words used, the shorthand, and the frightening phrases used in the headlines and in the newscasts at night were most disturbing. Surveys have shown that if people retain anything from an evening television news show it is something that has been repeated. The repetition of words like "epidemic" and "pusher" and "junkie" and "needle" tend to fix them and their connotations in people's minds.

Sometimes it appears that we are about to philistinize public policy. We must be very careful not to let that happen in the area of drugs.

The lack of attention that this report got is shocking. It is shocking the way it went right through the media mill in one day.

Apparently, it will be lost, except in places like the drug-abuse symposium. Among groups like that, the debate will continue, but until you can get it properly before the public on television, the task of coping with the drug problem will not be any easier.

The Power of Suggestion

ROBERT HUGHES

The National Commission on Marihuana and Drug Abuse found in its report that most efforts to stop the contagion of ideas that spreads drug abuse have been counter-productive. They have not worked because people did not know what they were doing when they took those actions.

Broadcast Media

Two years ago, in the spring of 1971, there was a record which was being played on many radio stations. It was a "catchy" little tune called "Once Over the Line" by Brewer and Shipley, two young folk singers. It mentioned Jesus and Mary, and there was the cryptic line, "One tote over the line." No one could ever get them to explain what they meant, but everyone assumed that because the word "tote" was associated with marihuana use, the song was about someone sitting in a railroad station, thinking about Jesus and Mary, waiting for a train, and smoking marihuana.

Shortly after the record came out, the FCC, through an order, notified broadcast stations all over the country that it had serious and pressing concern about the broadcast of records which the commission said tended to promote or glorify the use of illegal drugs such as LSD, speed, and marihuana. The immediate reaction from stations, especially stations that programmed progressive or regular rock, was to wonder why the commission had no pressing concern about records which promoted the use of alcohol—Frank Sinatra singing "Drinking Again"—or records which promoted the use of nicotine.

While doing a documentary on the question of whether rock music tends to promote or glorify the use of illegal drugs, an effort was made to trace the origin of the FCC order. About the time the order was promulgated, the military was having an immense problem with discipline in the service. Commanders found that for some reason they could not communicate with the young troops under their command. The familiar story was one of discipline breaking down and persons in Vietnam refusing orders to perform various tasks. The Pentagon has someone who is "hip" about what is going on in mass media, so they approached him and asked, "Can you do something to tell our commanders how to communicate with young soldiers?" The result was a presentation—slides, tapes, and live narration. One of the things he concentrated on was rock music, and he mentioned the fact that certain drugs were mentioned in rock music. Their names were pronounced and people were said to get high and "get it on."

The presentation was meant to show commanders that if they wanted to communicate with their troops they should consider using radio, newspapers, or posters. Military memos just would not get the message to them.

Eventually, the presentation found its way to broadcasters at the White House and then found its way to the FCC where Commissioner Robert E. Lee saw it. Commissioner Lee was very concerned at the time about pornography in broadcasting, and he became concerned about the apparent appeal to drugs, so he began doing some investigating. He was the individual who pushed the order that went out to broadcasters, which most broadcasters interpreted as an attempt to censor so-called "rock lyrics."

When asked what evidence he had, if any, that rock lyrics promoted the use of drugs, Commissioner Lee said that he had none, and that to his knowledge no one had done any scientific studies on the question. When asked why he thought the lyrics promoted drug use, he said, "Well, I remember in World War II when Kate Smith sang 'God Bless America,' and I think that helped us to win the war. If a song can do that, then perhaps 'One Tote Over The Line' can get somebody to try marihuana."

The presentation mentioned earlier went through considerable changes, depending upon the audience to whom it was presented. When the presentation was shown to some high school students, they played the Beatles song, "With a Little Help from My Friend." You could hear the singing, "I get high with a little help from my friend," and the narrator said, "The drug message in the song comes through loud and clear," and stopped. In a transcript of the same presentation given to broadcasters at the White House, the narrator said, "The drug message comes through loud and clear to you, whether they realize it or not," seeming to indicate that playing a record on the radio somehow triggers a mechanism in your head that causes you to take drugs. Yet, at the same time, there were no scientific studies whatsoever to back that up.

The person who designed some of the music programming for Muzak (Muzak claims that its music can motivate people to work better in factories) indicates that the basic part of music that works on people's psyches is rhythm and structure, chords and notes together. He said that lyrics have no effect whatsoever. That, he said, was the reason why Muzak used no vocal music in any of its tapes.

Anyway, the Drug-Abuse Commission found that rock lyrics dealing in any way, shape, or form with drugs were pulled off the air, including one very strong song which says, "Goddamn the pusher man." (In this country, a broadcaster is risking complaints from the FCC any time he allows the word "damn" or "hell" on the air. However, there were some stations in the country that felt there was a drug problem and, thus, a need for that record. But, it came off the air regardless.

The commission is going to publish an appendix which discusses the whole subject, which should be very interesting reading.

It may well illustrate the dangers of taking action before knowing exactly what effects the action will have.

Discussion

The front page of the *New York Times* carried a report that the commissioners met at the White House with the president and received a frosty reception. There was editorializing in the *Times,* which raised the topic, "How is this commission going to be received? What is really the attitude of those who are in a position to do something with the recommendations of the report? To zero in on that, whether the word "frosty" is used or not, you can realize that the kinds of recommendations made in the report are new, different, novel, and bound to be, in some sense, controversial. One of the reasons for that is that there is much public concern about crime and the relationship between crime and drug use. The Consumers Union disagrees with the commission, in terms of the effect or effectiveness of certain treatment approaches, such as methadone maintenance, in lowering or reducing the rate of urban crime.

What has the commission found and what questions have they raised about the relationship between crime, drug use, and drug abuse?

> The National Commission on Marihuana and Drug Abuse disagrees with some of the findings that the Consumers Union made. When we looked at the treatment programs around the United States, we were very much concerned because there is now a tendency to lean on methadone maintenance as a panacea. We really know very little about how good such

programs are if the goal is to cure the addict or reintegrate him into the society.

One of our problems is that we have a whole range of programs, none of which has really systematically been evaluated. The Special Action Office is trying to evaluate those programs. Such an evaluation is long overdue. The original intent of Drs. Dole and Nyswander when they put together methadone maintenance was not to cure crime or to reduce crime; it was to help the individual by getting him maintained and stabilized so that they could do something with him in terms of job counseling, in terms of reintegrating him, and in terms of making him a functioning member of society. It was only when people started noticing that crime seemed to decline that it shifted from a concept of helping the individual toward a policy of law enforcement and control.

The studies that have been done with methadone are normally before-and-after studies, and there are considerable statistical aberrations in them. The commission tried to point out some of them. There is no question that the methadone programs have some impact on the reduction of crime, but how much is unknown. The next question is whether that is the only thing that is important. The Consumers Union talks about an experimental heroin maintenance program to test whether or not methadone is the best drug to use for maintenance purposes. There is no such thing as an experimental heroin maintenance program. If you are going to allow people to inject the drug and if you are going to give them heroin, forget methadone maintenance.

As to the experiment in England—we have done studies in England, one of which we completed this year. We have been there and there is no question of what the drug of choice is going to be; it is going to be heroin. There is no question about the drug of choice in terms of methadone administration; it is going to be injection. If your primary concern is the reduction of crime, the answer is very simple—give the addict the drug and he will not go out and steal.

However, that may not be the complete answer either. We did a cohort study, rather Dr. Wolfgang did, in Philadelphia. The test group was comprised of all boys born in the city of Philadelphia in 1945. From that and other studies we found that well before subjects went on to use heroin, they had run-ins with the police, were delinquent, and generally had been "criminogenetic." The real question is whether treatment of the symptom is going to relieve the criminality. It might reduce the property crime, but what about the assaultive crime? No one knows the answer to that question. Those very simplistic solutions of, "Well, that is going to eliminate crime," are just that; they have not been tested. We are very hopeful, but we certainly do not have the answer.

You have to be realistic when you talk about heroin maintenance, and you make the decision for yourself. The commission does not support heroin maintenance, but it does support methadone maintenance. However, we feel that there is no doubt that heroin will supplant methadone if it is given as a treatment modality.

Also, there is a cultural difference between the United Kingdom and America which accounts for the difference in drug use in the two countries. We have a much higher index of heroin incidence in this country and it appears that we will continue to have a higher incidence. We also have a higher incidence of burglaries and a whole other range of criminal activities. Our reference to Japan was a reference to dealing with a drug problem singularly, focusing on only one drug at a time.

Our response is that those countries where there is widespread availability of the drug at a cheap price—such as in

Thailand, Hong Kong, and the United Kingdom—have a wide range of drug use and drug dependence within their populations. The estimate of drug dependence within Hong Kong is approximately twenty per cent of the male population between sixteen and twenty-five. Whether that is good or bad is a subjective judgment. Whether the people can function or not is another subjective judgment, because "functioning" is a subjective term.

However, it is clear that one does not just focus on property crime and then worry about whether there is going to be a black-market. One does worry about availability because every time a drug is opened up there will be availability. We are not talking about marihuana here; we are talking about a highly targeted drug, one to which certain populations are highly vulnerable. Based on those considerations, we feel that policy making, not merely logic and philosophy, must play a role in any availability decision. Policy makers must speculate about an increase in drug use and the consequences of availability. It is a legitimate concern. As long as there are serious questions about it and there is comparative data to weigh, you have to be cautious. Once you have built a cultural context in which people can use drugs or receive drugs, it is a very difficult thing to change.

So you should not keep looking at the facile argument that heroin maintenance is going to reduce crime because it will not. In the commission's judgment, there is no such thing as an experimental heroin maintenance program.

Michael R. Sonnenreich

There is, of course, except in the case of a very few addicts, no cure and, indeed, the euphemisms that are used—treatment, rehabilitation, sometimes cure—are unfair. They are unfair to the addict and they are unfair to the rest of society.

At the end of 1971 in England, 1,161 of the 1,555 registered addicts were receiving methadone. Of those, 229 were also receiving heroin, 156 were receiving heroin either alone or in combination with other drugs, and 238 addicts were getting still other drugs. What has happened in the United Kingdom, where there was essentially an all-heroin population, could also happen in the United States. In the United Kingdom, heroin has become virtually a trivial drug and methadone is the maintenance drug of choice.   *Jonathan Leff*

What you have to say when you use those figures is that something like eighty per cent of the methadone is injectable and, therefore, indistinguishable in effect from heroin—so you are really talking about an injectable.   *James Markham*

In the United Kingdom, society does not find it reprehensible for an addict to inject the drug.   *Jonathan Leff*

I am not talking about reprehensibility; I am talking about the kinds of drug you are using. "The British are turning over to methadone" argument is really a distortion of the situation.   *James Markham*

We believe that the experimental testing should include testing injectable drugs against themselves and against oral drugs as well.   *Jonathan Leff*

One thing I wish we could stop—and I do not know how to do it—is the making of comparisons to the British experience. The situations are incomparable.   *Sander Vanocur*

The United States and Britain started with the same base and we went one way and they went the other. Of course, we have a large heroin population here—we have been maintaining a black-market for close to sixty years. *Jonathan Leff*

But the British have a totally different approach to crime and violence.   *Sander Vanocur*

How did it affect your work to be on a presidential commission—a commission that was started by the president but to which he has become very unreceptive?

First, it is a congressional commission. Presidential commissions are created by executive order. We were created by statute in the Comprehensive Drug Abuse Prevention and Control Act of 1970.[16] It is a bipartisan commission which means there are Democrats and Republicans on the commission. (No American party members.) We have four congressional members: two from the Senate—Senator Harold Hughes, a Democrat, and Senator Jacob Javits, a Republican; and two from the House—Congressman Carter, a Republican, and Congressman Paul Rogers, a Democrat. The nine other members were appointed by the president, but they, too, are bipartisan. It is generally referred to as a presidential commission because the majority of the members were appointed by the president, but that is not unusual.

As for the unreceptive reaction, it matters little. Since the subject is controversial, initial reaction does not concern me terribly. If you look back at the history of the Prettyman Report of 1963 and *The Challenge of Crime in a Free Society* in 1967, you will find that most of the recommendations, in time, get adjusted.

We are not terribly interested in having every single recommendation of the commission adopted. What we want is for

16. Comprehensive Drug Abuse Prevention and Control Act of 1970, 84 Stat. 1236 (codified in scattered sections of 21, 42 U.S.C.).

people to start rethinking the issue and rethinking the basic assumptions. If that is done, we can all disagree legitimately, but first, at least, let us agree on certain logical sequences.

Michael R. Sonnenreich

What are the medical advantages of addiction to methadone vis-a-vis heroin? And is it true that it is much harder to withdraw from methadone than from heroin?

Methadone is fully effective by mouth, which does away with all the needle-connected disease conditions; it is effective for a full twenty-four hours; it is effective in stable doses with minimal side effects and with safety, effectiveness, and acceptability already proven under actual field conditions with some 85,000 addicts.

Jonathan Leff

There is a basic difference. Heroin by mouth is ineffective. You have to use it by injection. There are two forms of methadone treatment in the United States today. One is the saturation dose of about 130 milligrams in your orange juice. That is a very high dose. In other words, you saturate the person. It would be much more difficult to bring a person down from that dose level than it would be for the average run-of-the-mill heroin-dependent person. There is another dose that is being used with increasing frequency—thirty milligrams. Unfortunately, you can overshoot the thirty milligrams, and that is one of the concerns of the Bureau of Narcotics and Dangerous Drugs. In other words, it is not a blockading dose at thirty milligrams.

It is true that you can also overshoot at 130, but it is a little harder to overshoot and get an effect when you are hitting at 130 milligrams a day.

Michael R. Sonnenreich

When one is on maintenance, you do not seek to bring him down, to withdraw him. That is detoxification. Maintenance means that you are maintained on a dose.   *Jonathan Leff*

I agree with you from a medical point of view. One of the problems, though, is whether people are going to overshoot. That is where you must blend the medical and the law enforcement considerations.   *Michael R. Sonnenreich*

You mentioned several studies of comparisons, cross-national research, and certain availability concepts in other societies. Have you done any studies of persons who have gone from one availability context, say, the New York ghetto, to another availability context, such as England? How does the American "hustle" (you alluded to that briefly) produce a reaction in a different kind of cultural environment?

We have not done a study of that, but we have the classic study of the American serviceman in Vietnam who was "addicted" and who came back into his own environment in the United States. There is no question about it, part of the reason some persons choose heroin rather than alcohol is, in part, the "hustle." There is a lifestyle that is involved with heroin use and it is not just a question of people saying, "I like this drug just for its effect." Many persons like the drug for its effect, and, crazy as it may sound, they also like that very undirectional approach to life. They have only one major goal—to shoot up every day—and the question is: How do you do it? So, this is part of the "hustle."
     Michael R. Sonnenreich

This focuses on another problem involving maintenance. When you maintain a person, you are trying to create a tolerance level so that he does not get high any longer but is still on the drug. When you start talking about heroin maintenance, you start getting into the question of whether a person should be allowed to shoot up and get high while he is being maintained or in treatment. What is your point of view?

We want highs, but we want you to take *our* highs. One of the things you notice when you start looking at methadone maintenance programs is that there has been a rapid growth of liquor stores around the clinics. You cannot walk into most of Bedford-Stuyvesant or such other areas without seeing that the addicts being treated take their methadone and then go next door to get bombed. There is a substitution. It is an obvious substitution and one of the interesting studies that the commission has not performed—I hope someone else will. I would like to see how many persons we are taking off heroin and putting into the alcoholic category.

Michael R. Sonnenreich

Methadone is a work-ethic drug. It does not answer the problem of some persons saying, "I do not want the work ethic. I do not want life the way it is supposed to be." I am not deploring this, nor am I putting the methadone thing down, but that is the way it is. The goal is to make useful citizens out of people on methadone. *Sander Vanocur*

There is a caveat here. There is a sort of willingness to believe that persons who are stabilized on methadone do not experience a high. It is anecdotal and perhaps unreliable, but there are addicts who will say that that is not exactly the truth. It is perhaps perceived by those who would remedy the ills of addicts as a work-ethic drug. But it may not, in fact, be quite as neat as Dr. Dole, and many people who have come after him in this field, would have us believe. In fact, there are many persons on methadone who do get high.

James Markham

You mentioned the fact that a certain number of heroin-dependent individuals are essentially copping out of an effective way of life. What percentage of heroin-addicted persons are willing to accept a methadone maintenance program?

Who knows? Realistically, we do not even know how many heroin-dependent persons there are in the United States. You may want to apply the famous rule of three—look at how many people are listed on the Bureau of Narcotics and Dangerous Drugs (BNDD) records as being addicts, then take the New York Registry and multiply it by three on the assumption that you only catch one in three—or you may want to apply a fish-in-the-sea theory. Since we do not know how many, I obviously cannot give you a percentage of how many want to use methadone. One answer would be clearly that it is not going to be all of them. In any event, for the ones that would come into the program, the real question is whether they are the most antisocial—I believe "antisocial" is a legitimate word since we are talking about the social norm. If you think methadone is going to be the panacea, you are wrong—it is not.

Michael R. Sonnenreich

Has the commission made any recommendation regarding the mode of administration of drugs? For example, if marihuana were legal, would it then be legal to inject tetrahydrocannibinal intraveneously?

No, we made no recommendations as to the mode of drug administration. I am personally not terribly impressed with the suggestion that the method of administration is at all crucial. As to the tetrahydrocannibal, our recommendations about cannabis do not apply to it. We were talking about natural products; we were not talking about synthetics. Obviously, every time you inject something you will get a faster reaction. In addition, there are inherent dangers in using hypodermic syringes, but we do not make recommendations as to that.

One thing that I have noticed is that we are talking about a lot of little specifics. You are doing what I hoped you would not do—talking about the little nits and picks that may be nice and interesting in terms of resolving little questions. But they do not get at any of the fundamental issues.

Michael R. Sonnenreich

One concern I have is that so far today we have discussed two models, the medical model and the therapeutic model. The Consumers Union, in its book, mentioned three models: the sociological, the psychological, and the medical. Yet, they never dealt with the sociological model. Has there been any kind of consideration of that model, in light of the often repeated claim that what we need is a solid prevention program which focuses upon the social and economic conditions that control people's lives?

We discussed the three approaches, as I mentioned, but we did not dwell on them because we feel it is more important how the addiction manifests itself.

There are environments in which some addicts apparently are able to maintain abstinence, for example, Synanon, which is very well known. The head of Synanon has remarked, as we reported in our book, that when ex-addicts leave the confines of Synanon, within two years ninety per cent of them are back on heroin. The alternative would appear to be that the addict must choose either to remain in Synanon or to return to heroin.   *Jonathan Leff*

First, it is said that certain things are o.k. if they do not affect anyone else. For example, you said smoking cigarettes is o.k. since if one wants to end up with a lung that hangs down to his knee, it is his own business. I assume, likewise, if one wants to use drugs, that is his own business. Why is it that you decide that getting high is *your* business?

Second, I do not understand why you are perpetuating this myth about methadone. Clearly, from what you have stated today, it would take a lot longer to get off methadone than it does to get off heroin, just physically. The only advantage that I have detected so far is that one does not have to use a needle. Studies have shown that people in factories have been able to work on heroin as long as they had money enough to maintain their habit. People on methadone are able to work, too. What is so great about not having to use a needle?

> There is an advantage of methadone over heroin—it lasts for twenty-four hours in oral form. For whatever reason, society by and large does not like the idea of people shooting things into their veins unless a doctor does it for them. This is a hangup and perhaps it is a wrong hangup, but it nevertheless is real.
>
> You are saying, "Why do we object to a high?" The answer is that we do not object to a high. We are concerned about structuring the high along more acceptable channels. You may think it is fine to be high on a particular drug. We looked at it, and we recognized that drugs are used for mood alteration. The question is how many can you use and how many can society sustain.

Most societies accept a drug, or several drugs. The question that we had to answer from a policy point of view was: What should be the category of drugs or class of drugs that we think people can get high on? We understand that people get high. No one is objecting to people getting high.

Michael R. Sonnenreich

My first point was that you and the commission appeared more concerned about the drugs which people are taking and the attitude that has developed than you were about the deaths that might result from cancer caused by cigarette smoking.

That was not our function. I am also terribly concerned about mental retardation, but that problem was also not within the scope of the commission's work. We were supposed to be dealing with this one particular area. What we are and were concerned about can be seen in the history of drug use and its place in our society. Most societies accept drug use of one form or another and they structure it. We happen to be a highly mobile, highly affluent society and do not have all the institutional controls which structure drug use in other societies.

The commission took the attitude that while others may worry about problems at the high end of the scale of drug behavior—the intensified, the compulsive use—we would concentrate on the structuring of the other kinds of use.

Michael R. Sonnenreich

It sounds as if we are right on the verge of letting the over-all pressures of society dictate, in a sense, or guide what law and medicine decide to do with the information. Society does not approve of people shooting things into their veins, and society does not approve of them getting high from their medicine—which is the result of maintenance programs. We really ought to think

about how much those kinds of pressures and the Puritan, if you will, standards of our society will influence: (1) the drugs we choose to maintain people with, and (2) the method or the style in which we let them take them.

> These basically are two of the points we were trying to make in the report. The most important recommendation we have is to change attitudes and ways of looking at drug use.
>
> But make no mistake about it, anyone who says, "Well, that is a Puritan ethic; Max Webber is dead," is being highly unrealistic because you do not make policy in 180 degree sweeps. You make policy at 110 and 120 degree turns. You can be in the vanguard, and you can take a couple of steps ahead of people, but then you had better be absolutely certain that you draw the people through an attitude change to your position so that you can proceed to the next change.
>
> We are not a country that works in radical sweeps. That is, perhaps, one of our strengths; it is also one of our frustrations, but it is a very, very important point. We do not want public policy to flip, because if it flips in this area it can flip in another area. The thing about which the commission is most concerned is the practice of looking at the problem with blinkers on. It is a social problem within a larger social framework and every time you start pressing buttons because you think that this is morally justified or it is morally horrendous, recognize that you are turning a policy over and you had better be certain that it conforms with that whole larger area we are talking about. *Michael R. Sonnenreich*

Chapter 5

Advertising

At a cost of some $400 million in 1972, drug advertisers in the United States conducted powerful campaigns to sell their products, regardless of need or welfare. Public awareness of their influence and success has increased to the point where some critics recently advocated a ban on television drug advertising.

The dangers of this type of advertising have been identified as (1) a massive problem of misinformation, and (2) the promotion of a conspicuous consumption style of living. Of the two, misinformation has created the greatest amount of concern. Skeptics of regulation or self-regulation suggest that countercommercials on radio and television are the most effective solutions to the misinformation problem, because the only bodies that could enforce rules against drug advertising—the FCC and Congress—have simply sidestepped the responsibility.

The Author

Nicholas Johnson
Impact of Drug Advertising

Mr. Johnson was appointed by President Johnson for a seven-year term as federal communications commissioner beginning July 1, 1966. He is a Phi Beta Kappa graduate of the University of Texas and an honors graduate of their law school. He served as law clerk to Justice Hugo L. Black of the U.S. Supreme Court, and while at the FCC, he has written about broadcasting and other communications policy issues.

Impact of
Drug Advertising

NICHOLAS JOHNSON
Radio and television commercials put forward a particular philosophy, a particular point of view, a particular style of life that is echoed throughout the programs as well as the commercials. It makes no difference, really, what product is being advertised because all commercials are commercials for all products. Moreover, all programs are written by the same persons who write the commercials and are paid for by the same persons who are likewise pushing the same style of life, the same commercial products, the same values of conspicuous consumption, and the same material gospel.

If you study them, you get a sense of the extent and the degree to which radio and television commercials make a very persuasive case for why we should not try to achieve our full potential as human beings, why we should not pursue the fulfillment of individuality, personal growth, and why we should not attempt to mold a maturity born of confrontation with reality. What radio and television commercials are telling us is that deodorants and soaps and toothpaste and mouthwashes will increase our sexuality; they tell us that we are not supposed to experience our feelings of fear or anger or anything else. They say that there is something dangerously unacceptable about an occasional sleepless night and that our psychic states are solely a function of the chemicals that we ingest. Beer drinking lulls us into the state of witlessness that is the prerequisite for watching the programs—as

Nathan Williams has observed, television wants to keep you stupid so that you will watch it. The advertisers, meanwhile, want us to watch, drinking their product, the commercials which are telling us that beer is going to give us the gusto to climb a mountain or engage in some other vigorous pursuit.

Commercials

Without multiplying the examples endlessly, the point is rather obvious that the drug advertisers are telling us what they and their advertising agencies believe is the best way of promoting their product, and persuading us to buy it, regardless of our need, regardless of our welfare, regardless of the merit of the product.

There is a sameness about these commercials, even though they are talking about different products, that has helped to produce its own national anxiety. Sometimes the anxiety is related to the program as well. You may notice the number of headache remedies that are advertised during the evening news, as if that were somehow the way to deal with problems that you have just been watching. Uniformly these advertisements heighten our awareness of the tensions of living in what is really a very hostile environment for human beings and for individual growth—a somewhat neurotic society, one might say, a society that is cluttered with the value structure and with the products of the other corporate sponsors. These commercials argue that the fault and the difficulties that we confront as human beings trying to make a life for ourselves in the corporate state that is America today lie in our failure to adjust to their values, and that the way we may become "normal" is to take the drugs and other mind-altering chemicals that they offer.

Last year the drug industry spent some $400 million trying to get such a message across to the American people. That constitutes some thirty-five per cent of the wholesale value of the drugs.

Of that $400 million, some $300 million was spent on television advertising alone.

The wine and beer industries spent $100 million pushing their products; those investments have certainly paid off. Americans are spending at least $2 billion a year on their nonprescription drug habit and about $31 billion a year on the nation's number one hard drug by any measure, alcohol.

Public Awareness

The problems posed by the broadcast advertising of drugs have not gone totally unnoticed. Public awareness has increased, as evidenced in part by this very conference. Recently on public broadcasting there has been a show called *The Advocates.* It has a debate format, and one evening the subject was whether drug advertising should be banned. After the show, the audience wrote in to vote regarding the proposition. When the case *against* a ban on drug advertising was entered as forcefully as advocates could put it (of course, the case *for* a ban on drug advertising was also forcefully put forward), of the audience that participated, who had heard both sides of the argument, eighty-five per cent said they wanted a ban on drug advertising on television.

The National Council of Churches held extensive hearings on drug advertising and concluded that pharmaceutical ads "encourage the misuse and abuse of drugs."

The president's Commission on Marihuana and Drug Abuse also recommended limitations on drug advertising. Congress has begun to reflect that concern as well. Senator Nelson introduced a bill that would regulate drug advertisements in an effort to prevent deception, and Congressman Claude Pepper has at least threatened to introduce a bill that would ban drug advertising during the daytime hours in an effort to help in dealing with the problems of drug advertising to children.

In short, I think that more and more Americans are becoming aware that they are living in a drug culture, one that is fostered by corporate avarice, one that has spawned an ever-increasing barrage of drug messages which encourage us to participate in the chemical lifestyle from which the drug companies profit so handsomely.

Problems

There are at least two major problems inherent in the content of these drug ads. There is a considerable danger that the constant airing of only one side of this particular question of science, of religion, of lifestyle, of philosophy has created a massive problem of misinformation on the part of the American people. Such misinformation is a problem in any society that is premised on democratic principles. It is especially serious when the misinformation happens to relate to the nation's health. Basically—and this is something the medical profession ought to be interested in—the drug advertisements are encouraging people (1) to be much more conscious of symptoms than they might otherwise be, and to be perhaps unduly concerned about their health; (2) to evaluate and note the particular symptoms which they have; (3) to diagnose their own ills; and (4) to prescribe their own pills. Why someone hasn't thought to bring a malpractice of medicine suit against the drug advertisers, I don't know, but that is essentially what they are engaged in—endeavoring to substitute their television commercials for the counsel of a doctor.

The second major problem is that the drug advertisements, like all other commercials, promote a conspicuous consumption style of life, which has geopolitical implications of international politics, as well as psychological implications, and such advertising is a major part of the responsibility for the kinds and degree of anxieties that we now see in Americans, which have led them to the chemical solutions in the first place. On the one hand, we give advertisers free rein to create an artificial demand for useless or harmful products, and at the same time, we limit the right of those opposed to get their message on the air. What you may not know is that the same persons who control the programs and the commercials also control the so-called public service spots through the Advertising Council which clears public service announcements for viewing on television. The council, as you might guess, is comprised of the very same persons who write all the other commercials. That is one reason why the public service spots you see say so very little about so very much.

It is the first problem, that of misinformation, which has spawned the greatest amount of public and congressional criticism so far, but the second problem is also now beginning to demand some serious attention. That is the problem that troubles the drug industry the most, because that industry literally thrives on the sorts of anxieties that are inherent in a consumption-oriented society, the kinds of anxieties that come from an individual's feeling of inadequacy because he is not consuming as much as that guy in the commercial. If you notice, virtually all of the commercials and the programs come to you from the $125,000 homes in which most Americans do not live.

It is always amazing to me that if you just turn on the television at random, you cannot tell, at first glance, whether it is a commercial or a program into which you have tuned. Take the typical Hawaiian beach scene—there is a man and a woman in an automobile on the beach and the waves are coming up on the sand. It may be one of those Hawaiian cops and robbers shows or it may be a commercial, but if it is a commercial there is no telling what it is going to be a commercial for. It may be for the airline that got them there; it may be for the automobile company from which they bought the car or the rental car company from which they rented it, or the hair spray company that provided the lady's hair spray, or the soft drink that is about to come bounding out of the waves. Or take the all-purpose commercial in which the lady walks out into the living room, which has expensive drapes, thick carpet, and expensive furniture. She is wearing a long dress and lots of makeup and hair spray. You do not know what she is going to sell you because it could be any one of those things, but then she takes out from behind her back a can of lemon "something" and sprays it all over. Basically what she is selling you is that $125,000 house and all that goes with it, and she says, "If you are not living this way, you do not amount to anything as a human being and you are unhappy and miserable because you do not have all this stuff that I have, and all that I have to wax and clean and move and dust and get repaired."

Well, in any event, that is why the broadcasting and drug industry so fear the prospect of information leaking out to the American public, and so it was that they groped for an instant cure for the congressional anxieties that had begun to reflect public worry about drug advertising. The National Association of Broadcasters' Code Review Board recently presented the public, and more particularly Congress, with a superficial remedy to the drug advertising problem which was reminiscent of the drug industry's simple minded remedy of the pill for every ill.

The National Association of Broadcasters, known in Washington as "NAB," has set out to nab the pushers, who turn out to be its own members.

Regulation

The new rules of the Review Board, the code, encourage broadcasters to regulate drug advertisements in a variety of ways. It encourages drug advertisements that provide factual information; it attempts to discourage advertisements that a product will alter the user's mood; it encourages drug advertisers to advise users to read the label. It seeks to prohibit the on-camera taking of pills, the use of children in drug advertisements, drug advertising that is adjacent to programs principally designed for children, and personal testimonials by celebrities.

The public ought to be extremely skeptical about this alleged effort at "self-regulation." First, even if those so-called rules were applicable to all stations, which they are not, and meaningfully enforced, which they are not, they are extremely vague and not even designed to correct anything but a small part of the problem.

The thrust of the drug advertisements is not likely to be changed—"Better Living Through Chemistry" is not just a DuPont slogan—nor is there any hope that the new rules will reduce the potential for misinformation inherent in such ads, nor is there any prospect for fewer drug ads, nor is there any hope for information about drugs from a source other than the pusher.

Misinformation

The only real answer to the problem of misinformation is to allow what are called "countercommercials" on radio and television. For example, when a drug commercial says that a particular aspirin product cures headaches faster than any other, the counter ad might offer the evidence that all aspirin is the same and that the least expensive brand is the best buy. Needless to say, the NAB code would have nothing to do with a proposal for counter-commercials.

Bayer was once using the American Medical Association's report that all those modified analgesics actually do you no more good, and in some instances more harm, than plain aspirin. Bayer, of course, did not use the entire report; it only used the report up to that point and then went on to say that, therefore, one should buy Bayer. A public interest group wanted to take the entire report, which went on to say that if you are buying aspirin, you ought to get the cheapest brand, and run that as a public service advertisement. The report does not go far enough. The public ought to be told why it is that you get headaches, what you can learn from headaches, how you can change your life so that you don't have any, and how massage works better than aspirin when you get one. The general counsel of the National Association of Broadcasters was asked why it was that he found the ad from Bayer quite acceptable but the ad from the public interest group, using the same information, unacceptable. He responded quite candidly that the public interest group's commercial would be, in his words, "too credible." In that regard, broadcasters are well aware that counteradvertising regarding cigarettes did far more to reduce the consumption of cigarettes in the United States than the ultimate ban on cigarette advertising.

The reason why the NAB solution cannot deal with the misinformation problem is because it relies upon the pusher to tell the truth about his product, a belief which remains a pipedream. In any event, the code doesn't deal at all, and never tried to, with the problem of drug orientation in our society, because a resolution of that problem would require either that all sides of the issue be heard or that drug advertising be banned entirely. A system of full information to the consumer has always been an anathema to the American businessman because he is frightened of the effect that intelligent choices in the marketplace might have on his merchandising efforts. He does not always agree that a fully informed consumer would continue to buy the best product in the marketplace, that free market forces would work, and that the free enterprise system would prevail.

It might very well be that a ban on drug advertising would increase the profits of drug companies. After all, they have a $300 million investment in advertising. It is interesting to note that after Wall Street understood the significance of the cigarette-advertising ban, stock prices shot up, not down. Cigarette consumption has begun to rise once again, now that people are no longer constantly reminded that cigarette smoking is associated with death as well as with sexuality and the other attributes of a fun-packed adult life.

Even if the regulations did offer a solution to the misinformation problem, which they do not, they would still be ineffective. If you have studied the process of so-called self-regulation by American industry, and if you have any misapprehension about its effectiveness, consider the situation in the broadcasting industry. In the first place, most broadcasters in America do not even subscribe to the NAB code. Only 3,000 out of 8,000 radio and television stations do so. Therefore, you have got 5,000 at the outset that are not affected by it at all.

Violations

What about the 3,000 that are affected? First, the code makes no effort to monitor what they do, so there is no way to report any violations that might occur, if they did occur. Second, if violations were reported, there is no method of fact-finding or hearing procedure which could be used to determine what the broadcaster actually did. Even if there were such investigatory procedures available there is still no procedure for the enforcement of regulations and there are no penalties attached to a violation. It is not surprising, therefore, that the NAB, as a protector of the public interest, is scarcely even a paper tiger.

The only bodies that could enforce rules against drug advertising are the FCC and Congress, and they will not. The FCC has simply abdicated its responsibility in this area, as it has in so many others. Congress, which once appeared concerned about the problem, has now been mollified by the broadcasters' superficial proposal of self-regulation. Congressman Paul Rogers, chairman of the house Public Health and Environment Subcommittee, has commended the broadcast industry for its new rules. "Certainly," he said, "this is a preferable way to handle matters, to let industry regulate itself where possible." And so it would appear that NAB has, indeed, scored a major public relations coup. Congress has cooled considerably in its attempts to do something about the still very serious problem of drug advertising.

Public Influence

The advertising, drug, and broadcasting industries have taken the pressure off Congress and, as *Broadcasting* magazine (the lowest common intellectual denominator for the industry) has characterized it, "We have headed them off at the pass."

What is disturbing about all of this is that those industries appear to have achieved their goal at such a very modest cost, with so insignificant a gesture, which is simply another indication of how powerful they really are. The American people, however, may not be fooled so easily in this day of shell games from Washington. In the final analysis, it is the people who do have some power to effect a change in drug advertising, but only if they will exercise that power, only if they will let their elected representatives in the House and Senate know that they, as well as the drug companies, intend to be heard on this issue. They must let their representatives know that they do not believe the issue has gone away simply because NAB has come up with a superficial, quick, fast-relief remedy in the form of its own code. Once elected representatives begin to understand that people do care about this issue, that they are going to hold them accountable on it, we may get a fair shake.

Discussion

Would you comment on the sponsors of the drug-abuse symposium?

I am always very interested in where money is coming from, because I find that there tends to be some correlation between the money that comes in and the result that comes out. The best way to deal with that is just not to take any of their money and thereby retain as much independence as you have. It is simply another indication of the far-reaching power of these industries, that even when we get together to discuss the problem, we go to them for money, and those who expect to go back and get money again obviously are going to be affected in some degree by what they say during the course of the conference. But then, that is the great American way and there is a lot right with America.

Would you explain why the FCC has abdicated its responsibilities, and perhaps talk about why and how it has done this?

The how is very easy; it just doesn't do anything. The why is more interesting. Most governmental agencies are carrying out industry's wishes rather than being engaged in any meaningful form of regulation. That is an overgeneralization, but it is basically accurate.

Would you comment whether you approve of advertising in medical journals?

I do not read the medical journals regularly, but I understand that they are full of drug advertising and that the drug industry spends approximately $5,000 per doctor, encouraging doctors to prescribe drugs. That seems to be rather excessive. Think of the medical care programs you could have in this country if you would take $5,000 per doctor and spend it on taking care of people instead of drug advertising.

There was a poll recently done among doctors in Boston, and some eighty per cent felt that doctors were overprescribing drugs.

The medical profession has the same kind of information problem about drugs that the public has. They are overburdened; there is a limit to how many of the thousands and thousands of research reports that come out every year they can read, and, to the extent that their minds get cluttered up with what they read in a full-page ad in a journal somewhere, it makes it more difficult to get factual information from any direction—a tremendous advantage to the drug companies in pushing their products. Our drug problem exists on many levels. The so-called drug problem and the over-the-counter problem are not the only ramifications of this. It is also present with the prescribed medicines.

Whenever you use not just a chemical, but a product of any kind, whether it is prescribed or not you affect yourself psychologically. It makes you less of a person. It says that you cannot deal with your own problem. You have got to go to an authority figure; you have got to go to something outside yourself to deal with it. Who you are and what you are is a function of how you look, what products you associate yourself with. We can see this throughout alcohol consumption patterns. People choose what they drink based on their image of self and the image they wish to project. They choose cigarettes on the same basis. They choose a whole range of products on that basis.

This is not to say that under no circumstance should you use any medicine. But when you prescribe medicine, either as a doctor or when you prescribe it for yourself as a patient by over-the-counter drugs, or when you get into other drugs like alcohol, basically you are getting away from yourself rather than into yourself. You are weakening your own selfhood and retarding your own striving toward a sense of potential and fulfillment, because you are saying that you can't deal with whatever problem you may have by yourself. This is one of the reasons why one of the most effective approaches to drug abuse that has come along has been something like the Maharishi transcendental meditation or Yogi Bajan's yoga. Those things do help; those approaches say, look inside of yourself; there is something very special about you as a human being. They say that you are functioning in about five per cent of your capacity as a human being—your capacity to love, to be productive, to enjoy physical health and energy and vigor, to be creative in an artistic sense. You are functioning in about five per cent of your potential, and however you want to express it, whether you want to use the language of religion or of psychiatry, or whatever language you want to use to talk about this, there is something very special about you which needs to have a chance to flower, to develop and grow. That is why I would much rather see someone deal with a problem of stress and tension by using meditation than by using aspirin, not just because the aspirin may be chemically harmful in some way, but because the aspirin is cutting you off from something you need to know about yourself.

There is nothing wrong with feeling pain. Pain is a way of finding out what is going on inside of you. There are a lot of things you need to feel pain about in order to get from here to there. I mean, there is a reason for it, and if you feel angry or upset or jealous or frustrated, whatever you are down about, whatever you feel, feel that feeling and try to understand it and try to understand where it is coming from. Do not cut your body off at the neck so that you do not understand what is going on inside your body. You need to know what is going on there, and to the extent that you can deal with a problem by jogging and getting more oxygen into your brain, by massage, by meditation, by nutrition, by getting more and better sleep, by breathing fresh air, there are just tremendous advantages to you as a human being in terms of finding out who you are, what you can do, and what you are all about. There is a whole pattern of behavior that is being forced down upon you by corporations that profit from it. They need to manipulate you. They need to deprive you of your own individuality and worth and strength and striving as a human being. They need to treat you as a mass. They need to keep you watching television. They need you to consume their products. They need to develop your anxieties and tensions and sense of inferiority and worthlessness. They need to develop your sense of being a member of a mob and not being anything.

Jesse Jackson stands before his assembled group in Chicago every Saturday morning and starts off his marvelous performance of combination church service, lecture, music, community meeting, news, and whatever all it is, with a chant: "I am somebody." And they repeat that back. All of us need a little bit of that, not just those poor blacks who are beaten to death in the kind of life that they have in that part of Chicago where they are living. All of us need to remind ourselves, "I am somebody."

Television is trying to beat that out of you, and the drug companies are trying to beat that out of you. To talk about the drug problem as we do makes both too much and too little out of it. It is part of a much broader, much more pervasive, much more venal, much more serious, much more debilitating problem as today we watch the decline and fall of the American empire.

Chapter 6

Civil Liberties

Although civil liberties problems are not always clearly defined, there are certain basic issues which are evident today: (1) mandatory minimum penalties; (2) urinalysis method of drug-use detection; (3) pretrial preventive detention; (4) involuntary commitment to drug programs; (5) confidentiality of records; and (6) criminal justice diversion.

Truth in the field has been evasive, and drug laws have been enacted without adequate facts available. The person who may have suffered the most from these failings is the drug addict himself—society's reject. One view is that free trade in narcotics and legalization of drug use would eliminate most of the problems of criminal offenses and the high costs to society. In all debates, the questions concerning treatment are of overriding importance, and many believe the solution to society's dilemma rests largely on this issue.

The Authors

Mark L. Cohen
Civil Liberties Problems

Mr. Cohen, a graduate of Syracuse University and Boston College Law School, is a project director of the Drug Abuse Council in Washington. He has served as executive director of the Massachusetts Committee for the Advancement of Criminal Justice, and as deputy director of the Massachusetts Council on Crime and Correction. Mr. Cohen was an assistant attorney general for the Commonwealth of Massachusetts and served as law clerk to the chief justice of the Massachusetts Superior Court.

Nicholas N. Kittrie
What is the Truth?

Mr. Kittrie is professor of criminal and comparative law at the American University and director of the Institute for Studies in Justice and Social Behavior. He has done research at universities in England, Poland, Germany, Israel, and Egypt. Previously counsel to the Judiciary Committee of the United States Senate, Professor Kittrie is the author of *The Right to be Different: Deviance and Enforced Therapy.*

Joe Moss
Little Law is Good Law

Mr. Moss serves as chief of the Appellate Division of the District Attorney's Office in Houston, Texas. Before assuming this position, he served as capital prosecutor and chief of the Felony Division. Mr. Moss was influential in revising the criminal laws of Texas and has lectured in most of the law schools in Texas. He served for three terms as county attorney of Garza County at Post, Texas, where he also practiced law.

Thomas Szasz
The Case for Legalized Drug Use

Dr. Szasz is a psychiatrist and professor of psychiatry at the State University of New York (Upstate Medical Center) in Syracuse. He is the cofounder and chairman of the Board of Directors of the American Association for the Abolition of Involuntary Mental Hospitalization. Dr. Szasz is the author of over two hundred articles and nine books, including *The Myth of Mental Illness, The Second Sin, Ideology and Insanity,* and *The Manufacture of Madness.*

Henry Brill
Society's Dilemma

Dr. Brill serves as director of Pilgrim State Hospital, West Brentwood, Long Island. He served as first deputy commissioner of the New York State Department of Mental Hygiene and was vice-chairman of the Narcotic Addiction Control Commission of New York State. Dr. Brill is a Phi Beta Kappa graduate of Yale University and a graduate of their medical school. He was appointed by President Nixon to the National Commission on Marihuana and Drug Abuse.

Civil Liberties Problems

MARK L. COHEN

It is hard to know what you mean by civil liberties; people have different concepts of what they are. One way of looking at the problems, without trying to define "civil liberties," is to raise some issues which people ought to be thinking about. Liberals, for instance, look at the civil liberties problem in an interesting way. They see measures taken against addicts as a beginning step toward locking the door on addicts, throwing the key away, and writing them off as viable members of society. They always are interested in the kind of slippery-slope concept which says that if you start just a little bit with one deviant group, you start to move toward a totalitarian state, and that every measure proposed has civil liberties implications if it has something to do with the exercise of controls over addicts.

Conservatives, on the other hand, see all the fuss that liberals make about civil liberties as a way of undermining, neutralizing, or nullifying any of the good programs that are proposed to control addicts or provide treatment and rehabilitation for them. They see the liberal reaction as a great big fuss over nothing, that, if taken too seriously, will destroy the ability of the programs to do very much.

The kinds of proposals that are coming out of the administration in Washington, such as preventive detention and mandatory minimum sentences, obviously have civil liberties implications. The bill in New York proposed by Governor Rockefeller talks about mandatory minimums, doing away with plea bargaining, and doing away with the right to probation and parole for narcotic drug offenders, particularly sellers of drugs. The civil liberties implications of those things are clear.

Issues

There are two issues to be considered: (1) the current policies that are being proposed, and (2) the political and philosophical justification for those policies. The general trend is to attempt to stop drug use and to stop persons who use drugs from continuing to do so. The justifications for that have to be examined before we look at particular policy issues.

Sometimes the policy questions are affected by certain assumptions. One assumption, for example, is that heroin addiction causes criminal activity. Some of these assumptions have not been tested until very recently; some of them have not been called into question at all.

For a while, in the middle 1960s, liberals were saying, "All we have to do is decriminalize drug possession and we will not have a crime problem any longer, since the price of drugs is artificially high." At the Drug Abuse Council we presented a report to show that the drugs would cost actually very little, something like twenty-three cents, to support the habit of a narcotics addict, and that it is the law enforcement effort that drives the price up and is responsible for the accompanying rise in crime rate.

Conservative politicians and law enforcement officials dismissed that out of hand until recently. In 1968 there was a presidential campaign in which the key issue was law and order. Yet, over the next four years it looked as if nothing was happening to stop the rising crime rate. Just before the next election some of the officials who were vulnerable on the point of crime started talking about a solution they had—treat and rehabilitate narcotic addicts, exercise controls over them, and thereby stop the crime problem. A billion dollars were put into the Special Action Office and the goal was to get narcotic addicts into treatment.

Questions

Questions which should be answered are: (1) Are addicts dangerous to themselves, to the community in which they live, and to society in general? (2) Do current policies achieve the purpose of ameliorating whatever real harm results from drug misuse? (3) Is the emphasis on the distinction between the medical and nonmedical drug user misplaced and overemphasized? (4) Is it a mistake to believe addicts ever enter treatment programs voluntarily or without involuntary commitment? A related question is, does the fact of a law enforcement effort against drug supply and drug users have the effect of driving addicts to treatment? Officials in the Soviet Union have reported that only three per cent of the persons in mental hospitals were involuntarily committed. We can see that even without action taken through involuntary petition commitment against drug addicts there are lots of other ways in which coercion may take place. (5) To what extent are policies aimed at the drug problem a part of the general repression in the United States against deviants—persons considered to be undesirable?

Those basic problems can be related to the specific policy issues which now confront policy makers and legislators; the issues are: (1) mandatory minimum penalties; (2) urinalysis to detect drugs among school children (a policy that has already gone into effect in the military); (3) pretrial preventive detention of drug law violators (someone charged with a drug crime then would not have the right to bail; he would not get out in the community unless he could show that he would not be dangerous and there was not a risk of life); (4) involuntary commitment, not to an institution, but to a drug program, which could be an outpatient methadone maintenance program (there has been general disillusionment with involuntary commitment to institutions because it costs too much and no one really thinks it accomplishes very much for those addicts); (5) confidentiality of records (what is the role of the psychiatrist or treating physician with respect to the criminal justice authorities who are looking to get at an addict if they think he has committed a crime? Do they have to divulge the information that has been communicated in confidence in the physician-patient relationship?); and (6) criminal justice diversion (ordinarily this latter issue is not thought of as a civil liberties problem).

The current trend is to take people charged with drug crimes and, instead of prosecuting them or sentencing them, refer them to a drug treatment program. One of the reasons why this *is* a civil liberties problem is that, of persons charged with certain crimes, only twenty to twenty-five per cent really are ever locked up in jail. It is a major problem of the criminal justice system to know what to do with the seventy to seventy-five per cent left over. If you put them on probation, that does not really mean very much. If you have the medical community take the responsibility of providing treatment if they live by certain rules, then it becomes a form of involuntary commitment if they are persons who otherwise would not be locked up because you do not have the jail space, or you do not have the resources to do it. It would cost too much to lock up everyone, so you take persons who ordinarily would not be locked up and you refer them to a treatment program.

What is
the Truth?

NICHOLAS N. KITTRIE

The pursuit of happiness is considered a particularly human characteristic. Other beings are not concerned with a state of happiness. The question is, how far a man may go in selecting what he considers to be his particular state of happiness. May he pursue only the search that we determine for him or may he define his happiness in such terms that might cause us to view him as deviant?

Fact or Fiction?

Then there is the right of a citizen to be told the truth. Unfortunately, the drug field is the field of the "big lie." We have been told lies for a long period, and the question is, to what extent an enlightened citizenry is entitled to be told what the facts really are. It used to be that the government's policy was to demonstrate that the number of addicts was going down. In 1960 the United States government officially sent a report to the United Nations Commission which said that as a result of our drug laws, which were characterized as being very effective, we had a small number of addicts. In fact, we used to say that before the drug laws came into being—we were a country without prohibitions of narcotic laws until 1914—we had a million addicts. But now that we have strict narcotics laws, we claim to have only 45,000 addicts. Subsequently, the policy changed. Now it fits the government policy to say that there is a tremendous increase in drugs and the use of drugs. We are told that there were at least 700,000 military men who were using drugs in Vietnam. Now we are building a tremendous machine and the question is, which is the truth? Do these severe laws actually serve to cut down the use of narcotics or are they ineffective? What is the truth?

It is shocking that we enact drug laws in this country without knowing what the facts are. All you have to do is to examine the hearings of the committee which decided to pass the marihuana laws. You will discover that the Senate Committee held hearings which, while lasting about five days in total, could have been compressed into one half day. On that basis a law was passed which resulted in the criminalization of great segments of our society. So the question is, what is the truth and can we get to that truth?

Socioeconomic Groups

It is unfortunate that the drug-abuse symposium did not have a larger audience of blacks and Chicanos. There is a growing attempt on the part of some elements in our society to drive a wedge between some of those so-called deprived socioeconomic groups and American liberals. When Governor Rockefeller came up with his strong recommendations pertaining to drugs the liberals were the ones who cried out against them, because they saw them as an invasion of privacy. But talk to people in the ghettos. They are not even satisfied with what he wants to do. Some would like to have public executions. There is a real need for liberals and some representatives of the communities where drug use is rampant to discuss these problems. It may very well be that in the Chicano and black communities government efforts to control some of these substances may be taken as very promising. Yet, those steps could very well be steps toward abuse.

This is not unlike the conflict you may have in the black community regarding birth control. Some may view birth control as genocide, and some may take the position that birth control is essential to improve the blacks' lot sufficiently so that they can be a strong community. It is not the total number of children that is important to a minority. The important question is how many children are to be brought up and what role will they have in society? The same discussions regarding drug policies are very important.

Criminal Justice

When it comes to the drug addict, I do not see the need for social defense. We are dealing with behavior that criminal law has very little need to regulate. In fact, much of our concern in this field is the arbitrary creation of an illegal black-market in narcotics which has made it very profitable for some persons to derive great benefits at a great cost to society.

If you want to look rationally at criminal justice and ask what the proper limits on criminal sanctions are, when we should use them and when we should not, there are probably four major tests you should apply. One is, what is the type and the degree of the social harm? What, precisely, is the social harm presented by narcotics or by marihuana? You could consider the fear that there is a public danger, but the major danger posed by users occurs when they go out to seek money to buy narcotics that they cannot get in any other way. You might take the position that narcotics produce individuals who will rely on welfare, and thus increase the number of lazy bums in society. But it is doubtful whether that justifies stiff criminal sanction. Or you may say that we need to engage in criminal controls of narcotics because we are our brother's keeper, and that brotherly love requires that we not allow anyone to go that terrible route. Again, it is doubtful that we want to use criminal law to enforce brotherly love.

The second test for rational policy regarding criminal sanctions ought to be a consideration of the side effects which would flow from the use of criminal sanctions. How adverse would those side effects be? The side effects produced by regulation of marihuana and narcotics are terrible. Basically, that is a field which others have labeled as a kind of victimless crime. That does not mean that there are not persons who suffer from it, but it is usually the person who uses drugs who is likely to be the main victim and he is not about to inform against himself. So it is an area of victimless crime in which you usually end up with wiretapping, government informers, entrapment, and other forms of criminal enforcement which we do not like. One of the adverse side effects is that we take individuals who may be harming themselves, and we label them for life. An ex-drug addict finds it more difficult to get employment than an ex-offender.

The next question for rational policy ought to be: Can the criminal law be effective? If the criminal law cannot be effective, then we ought to consider whether we want to use it at all. In this field there is too much profit for criminal law to be effective. There is also too great a supply of narcotics for criminal law to be effective.

For example, the world production of opium amounts to 1,400 tons a year. It takes only about five tons to supply all the needs of the United States. That means we need only one-third of one per cent of the world production to satisfy our drug addicts. Therefore, even if you eliminate ninety per cent of the supply, you cannot control it. When there is that much profit, the little amount required to supply the American addicts will continue trickling in.

Some may say that criminal sanctions in this field do not work because the sanctions are too weak. In New York estimates are that only two per cent of those arrested for drug felonies go to prison. Do you want to turn around and say that we will get a big percentage of all the drug addicts into prison? The total number of spaces in our prisons amounts to 250,000. Yet, the National Commission on Marihuana and Drug Abuse tells us that two million persons in the country have used heroin. It tells us that four and a half million use cocaine. Do you want to get them all into prisons, or only the pushers, and who is not a pusher?

Studies definitely indicate how confused we are about the pusher. We think of the pusher as a fellow from the big city who goes to a nice little village and pushes; but the pusher is your friend. That's the truth. It is someone you know who offered you that drug the first time. The pushers are just people that we know. If we want to put them all into prison, we are going to fill the prisons; and if we want life sentences, and if we need to keep them in prison, then we might as well execute them all. There is no need to keep persons in prison for thirty or forty years at the cost that is involved. If we are really concerned that the danger and hazard is all that big, let's have the executions.

The fourth consideration should be whether there are other tools that are more effective than criminal sanctions, and whether there are some other tools that are more suited. The tools other than criminalization and strict criminal sanctions have been the following: (1) civil commitments for therapy (I have great difficulties with that because the cures are not easy and the cost is very high); (2) Drug maintenance (when we talk about drug maintenance we do not mean legalization but a government monopoly, where the government sells drugs to those that need them under certain controls); and (3) leaving drug addicts completely alone and allowing a free market in drugs.

As long as there is doubt, as long as there are questions about the hazards created by drugs, we should not go to the last option of having free traffic, but it seems wise to allow drug maintenance for those who will pay for it. I do not think they should get it for nothing. We do not get alcohol for nothing. There ought to be a kind of reasonable government price—make a little profit and use the rest for rehabilitation.

Little Law is Good Law

JOE MOSS

There is no human on earth being mistreated more by the law in this country than those who are associated in some fashion with drugs, from top to bottom—those that grow it, import it, transport it, synthesize it, advertise it, sell it, push it, use it, do with and do without it, including the physician, legitimate and illegitimate.

In the 1930s, when they passed the Harrison Act,[17] the people that were first prosecuted were doctors. It was not until later that we got around to the more civilized people and started prosecuting them, too.

Uniform Laws

We are mistreating persons in the drug business because our laws are not uniform. Whatever laws we are going to have, they should be made uniform. So it should be with murder, rape, thievery, anything else, and particularly with drugs. Unfortunately, none of us here is in a position to do anything about that. The making of laws often entails the process of buck-passing by individuals who quite often are not attorneys. You can ask one of our legislators about dope and what to do with a narcotics addict or pusher, and he will give you the gobbledegook that we need to get dope into the hands of legitimate physicians who can use it for a blessing to mankind, and that we need to keep it away from the pusher who is giving it to our little children. Just what would he mean and just what would he know?

Minimal Law

We can draw on our own experiences, and we should agree on a few things. The solution to the drug problem, like any other human problem, is ninety-nine per cent education. I do not think we are ever going to be able to do anything with it by law any more than we were ever able to do with alcohol by law. In short, "Very little law is very good law."

17. Act of Dec. 17, 1914, ch. 1, § 1, 38 Stat. 785.

The Case for Legalized Drug Use

THOMAS SZASZ

In a free society, all drugs, regardless of their dangerousness, should be legalized. Free trade in drugs is desirable for the same reasons that the founding fathers favored free trade in ideas. As in an open society it is none of the government's business what idea a person puts into his head, so it is none of its business what drug a person puts into his body. In other words, just as we regard freedom of speech and religion as fundamental rights, so should we regard freedom of self-medication as a fundamental right. Instead of mendaciously opposing or mindlessly promoting drugs, we should, paraphrasing Voltaire, make this maxim our rule: I disapprove of what you take, but I will defend to the death your right to take it!

To be sure, like most rights, the right of self-medication should apply only to adults, and should carry with it unqualified responsibility for the effects which one's own drug intoxication behavior has on others. Persons who commit criminal acts while under the influence of drugs should not only be held responsible for their conduct but, in general, should be punished more severely than persons who commit the same offenses while not under the influence of drugs.

Free Trade

The idea of free trade in narcotics frightens people, perhaps because they believe that vast masses of the population would spend their days and nights smoking opium or mainlining heroin, instead of working and shouldering their responsibilities as citizens. But this is a bugaboo that does not deserve to be taken seriously. Habits of work and idleness are deep-seated cultural patterns; I doubt that free trade in drugs would convert industrious people such as the Americans, the English, or the Germans, from hustlers into hippies at the stroke of a legislative pen.

Law Abuse

The other side of the coin regarding drugs and drug control is actually far more important. Our present policies toward the problems of drug abuse and drug addiction are actually inconsistent with our most cherished moral sentiments concerning personal freedom and responsibility; they gravely imperil our judicial and political institutions and the liberties they guarantee; they aggravate rather than ameliorate the so-called drug problem; and they are astronomically expensive to boot. In short, our problem is exactly the opposite of what it is generally claimed to be. The problem is not drug abuse, but rather law abuse. What is wrong, what is immoral and unconstitutional—what should be illegal—is not the taking of drugs by some Americans, but the presumption by the American government that it may tell us what drugs we can and cannot take, thus promoting, even compelling, us to take those it approves, and prohibiting and persecuting us for taking those it disapproves.

The prohibition of certain classes of drugs creates a brisk illegal traffic in them, just as did the prohibition of alcohol a half century ago. Furthermore, our present national craze outstrips anything attempted during Prohibition, for we now not only deliberately create an immense amount of criminal behavior among both the suppliers and the consumers of illicit drugs, but we also use tax monies to underwrite the so-called treatment of the nonexistent illness called "drug addiction." The result is that we declare drugs "public enemy number one," and wage a "war on addiction," thereby generating a popular delusion suggestive of such earlier crowd madnesses as the Crusades and the witch hunts.

The Constitution and the Bill of Rights are silent on the subject of drugs. Thus, when the American people decided to outlaw alcohol, they passed a constitutional amendment to do so.

That clearly implies that, as American citizens, we have a constitutional right to medicate our bodies as we see fit. It is time that we look more closely, not only at the effects of harmful drugs, but also at the effects of harmful laws.

In the history of mankind, many more persons have been killed by laws than by drugs.

Society's Dilemma

HENRY BRILL

When one deals with problems that come in small packages—individuals and families are in trouble—it is very difficult to offer either political or philosophical abstractions. People and their problems demand that something be done.

Treatment

There is a cure, and there are recoveries. Scientific studies have shown that even under the old system, somewhere in the neighborhood of forty per cent of the patients who went through Lexington and finally returned to New York City were clean twelve to fifteen years after their return. It is also true that twenty-five per cent were dead and that the rest were in and out of hospitals and followed a fluctuating course. However, to say that recovery is rare, even under the old system, is misleading.

Under methadone treatment, a conservative estimate is that, among hard-core cases, somewhere in the neighborhood of sixty to seventy per cent show a change of lifestyle and a successful and satisfying adjustment.

Information

We have heard statements about how little we know. They have to be interpreted carefully, however, because we know a great deal. The number of facts that have become available in the field of drug dependence in the last few years is incredible. Our lack of knowledge lies in our inability to interpret those facts and translate them into action.

The interpretation of the vast volume of information which is available is a frustration to those whose duty it is to formulate public policy. They are caught between civil liberties issues and the demands of agonized families and the public; it is not an easy position in which to be. Many of you will be in that position some-day, if the law does not change its nature. If you are lawyers, your attitude may depend on who your client is. If you are defending a patient, you may have one attitude. If you have a client with a family that is in distress because of the patient, you may have a different attitude.

Addiction and Crime

The question whether addicts ever turn to treatment volun-tarily has been raised. Sometimes they do and sometimes they do recover. They do not all have to be dragged in by the heels; how-ever, the number that comes in voluntarily is relatively small. The vast majority and those who are the most serious social problems do not come willingly.

This raises other questions: (1) what is there about the be-havior of the addict which makes it necessary to consider the use of coercion; and (2) is there a connection between addiction and crime? Anyone who has dealt with a number of addicts knows that there is a connection between addiction and crime; addicts are extensively involved in crime. Is there a connection between the detoxification process and a return to a better form of life? Of course there is. There is about a ninety-five per cent reduction in the amount of crime among successful methadone cases. That is hard to get around. Whether there is an effect on the over-all crime statistics is a separate issue to which no answer has been given convincingly.

We have several options open to us, when we are faced with an individual who is involved in criminal behavior which is connected to or associated with his drug problem. He can be handled on a strictly legal level; that has been done, but with poor results. Thrown into the lockup, the addict goes into "cold turkey" withdrawal; he gets sick. If he is thrown in with prisoners who really do not belong in the same classification, the results can be brutal. It goes against the grain to consider and treat as criminals persons who are, at least for a time, really sick in the true physical sense.

On the other hand, if one considers the addict as sick, that raises other issues. Is the state of dependence really an illness?

British System

There is a third option we might consider, and that is the so-called British system. There is no analogy between the British problem and our own. It is an error to say that Britain and America started off on the same footing a hundred years ago. The British had neither a narcotics problem nor a street problem until about 1964 or 1965.

The British heroin maintenance system provides the drug intravenously for the addict—entirely different from the American system. As long as intravenous opiate is available, oral methadone maintenance will be driven out by a species of Gresham's law. The addict will not take oral methadone, which gives him no bang, or very little bang, when he can get the bang he wants from the intravenous drug.

The problem in England apparently has been contained since they started to issue heroin through government-controlled clinics. The number of addicts has not escalated as rapidly as it had been in the period two or three years before the new program started. On the other hand, the behavior of those who are being maintained has not improved nor has the morbidity, mortality, and the way in which they take their drugs. For us to apply this system to

600,000 heroin users in the United States, which is one guesstimate, would be impossible.

Society's Dilemma

There is no question that it is easier to treat a patient where sanctions exist in the background. When an addict feels that his treatment is purely voluntary, he may be unable to control himself. Whatever that means, it applies only to the abstinence program. With methadone, the treatment can be entirely voluntary. In fact, it has to be entirely voluntary.

What society's decision will be in the face of this kind of dilemma is not known. But physicians in hospitals are not racing to take charge of the patients. They are reluctant to treat alcoholics, and they are even more reluctant to treat addicts, for a very good reason. They are difficult to treat and their treatment may have bad public relations repercussions. However, the problem is there and cannot be solved by rhetoric. We will probably move from one point to the next, and there will likely be some gradual development of a pragmatic technique.

There are pharmacological treatments in the wings right now which may make the opiate problem moot within ten years. That will not solve the other drug-dependence problems, but it could be that a good pharmacological approach will make the difference and will save the Constitution.

Discussion

When you look at persons who have been involved in a rehabilitation program or abstinence for a period, you can never know for certain whether the abstinence resulted from the rehabilitation program or whether the persons matured or otherwise got clean themselves.

Earlier studies of continued criminality among addicts involved in methadone maintenance showed that these individuals, for the most part, were not committing crimes when they were in the methadone maintenance program. The addicts who were part of those programs, however, were hand selected. Later studies indicate that the rearrest rate among individuals on methadone maintenance is almost as high as when they were on the streets. This is a very unsettling statistic because people looking at the addiction problem often assume that once addicts are brought into methadone maintenance programs, they will not continue their criminal activity. Also, individuals stabilized in methadone maintenance programs are probably less vulnerable to arrest.

Assuming that addicts are going to commit crimes regardless of whether they are dependent on a drug, what real interest do we have in spending a billion dollars to lock people in jail or to force them into treatment? What are the dangers to society that result from addiction?

> The general principle that addicts make more addicts has bothered communities. In a black community in New York where we proposed a pilot program with heroin, those highly experienced people told us bluntly: "Not in our neighborhood." The contagious quality of heroin use bothers every community where it has taken root. *Henry Brill*

Christians beget Christians and blacks beget blacks. But this leads us to the fundamental question of whether persons who take drugs are dangerous per se or whether they are dangerous primarily when perpetrating the crimes that secure funds for more drugs? The statistics seem to indicate that the major crimes committed by drug addicts are crimes to get drugs. Obviously, if they are put on methadone, they get their drugs at a government office and do not have to commit crimes to support their habits. Why wouldn't the principle be applicable to maintenance with heroin?

> It would take a while to explain the difference between methadone maintenance and the state of heroin addiction, but there is a world of difference. There is one important fact that you must realize. A state of chronic inebriation—inebriation in the usual sense—is undesirable. A basic objection to the taking of heroin intravenously, four or five times a day, is that persons associated with the addict—his family—object to having him in a state of chronic inebriation—chronically disabled. So, there is a human side to this thing. It goes beyond the crimes they commit.   *Henry Brill*

The position of some is to do away with the control of drugs and drug users. Are we talking about giving an addict an absolute right to obtain an uninterrupted supply of drugs? In other words, does any law enforcement effort to keep drugs from coming into the country cut down on the addict's right to use drugs in the same way the rest of us breathe the air?

If we are not talking about a completely free-market system, we are talking about a maintenance system. Do we realize that individuals maintained by physicians at some point are going to want to use more drugs than the physicians are going to allow? Physicians in England start to cut back on the dosage levels once they feel they are being successful in the rehabilitation process. This has resulted in a black-market problem in that country. You can have a certain number of addicts maintained on drugs, but some will go to the black-market for additional supplies. Therefore, we really have to realize that there are going to be social costs, in terms of increasing addiction, with either an interrupted supply of drugs or maintenance programs.

As a point of semantics, there would be no addicts because there are no addicts until someone calls them that and has the power of the law to impute that status to them. There are persons who take chemical agents. But there are no "addicts." Until we learn that, we will just produce confusion. The government may not like the chemical agent you may want to take. If that is the case, the government calls it a narcotic. If the government likes it, it calls it a food. It is that simple.

Methadone maintenance is a medical religion and the theology in it is the medical profession. Maintenance, however, is the disease. Methadone maintenance is the gas chamber to which the blacks go as willingly as the Jews went in Germany. The coincidence is not a coincidence.   *Thomas Szasz*

The large proportion of all methadone cases are white, not black. The original attitude in the black community was one of suspicion. However, it has now been accepted in one black community after another. It is recognized for what it is, a better way of living than that which it replaces.

If anyone has any doubts as to what the results of a free opiate market are, he should read the history of China, when opiates in their mildest form were on a free market. There were tens of millions of opium addicts and it took a revolution to solve the problem.   *Henry Brill*

In our jurisdiction, thirty per cent of the people are black and we simply do not have any drug problem within that group that is worth mentioning. We do have a drug problem with the Chicanos, though. Is there any relationship in the North between blacks and drugs?

I think the incidence of addiction here is considerably higher among the people in the ghetto.   *Mark L. Cohen*

It is very easy to look for so-called progressive labels and become caught in a bind. I understand the references to a malfunctioning member of the family, but what are you going to do about it? The fact that the individual is taking certain drugs may be merely incidental.

We are always looking for easy explanations for social problems. About ten years ago one explanation for criminality was that sixty or seventy per cent of all persons who were in prison were there because they had committed a crime while intoxicated. Today, we are told that sixty or seventy per cent of those in prison are there because they had taken drugs. Obviously, they are there because they were committing certain crimes, and while there may be many explanations, to attempt to attribute criminality to a group labeled that way may be very misleading.

We are told that we must respond to malfunctioning individuals with compassion. There were probably 30,000 to 50,000 persons dismissed from the Armed Forces simply because they were taking certain drugs. The lifelong stigma attached to these persons in the name of compassion appears very unsatisfactory.

There is also a strong movement these days to say that we really do not want to use criminal sanctions against persons who take drugs because they are brutal. The alternative being espoused is mandatory medical treatment. The question is whether there really is any difference between the two views.

Further, we really ought to ask whether there is such a thing as rehabilitation. Not only is there no such thing as medical treatment in this field, but there is also probably no such thing as rehabilitation in the criminal field. You can detoxify someone, you can dry him out, but what is waiting for him when he gets back to society? Is there going to be a job for him? Is there going to be a place for him to live? Those are the key questions, and treatment is not the magic solution.

Nicholas Kittrie

In spite of opposition to mandatory minimal sentences, it looks as if mandatory minimals will be enacted in New York. Whether plea bargaining, parole, and probation for the drug offender will also be eliminated is still an open question.

Urinalysis—to protect drug usage in schools—is another area of concern, and there is opposition to that. Pretrial preventive detention—uniformly, everyone objects to it. Involuntary commitment of any sort also meets with opposition. Pretrial diversion is an option that many are now looking to with greater favor.

The whole debate has been shifted. For a while people thought they really could talk about decriminalization. Now they say that the best thing we can do is take persons who have been arrested for various crimes—not only drug crimes—and refer them to treatment instead of prosecuting them. That may be the humane option which is available within our political context.

> We may agree about treatment, but I am not going to do it; you are not going to do it; the policeman is not going to do it; the doctor is not going to do it; the mother and father are not going to do it. Who is? If you can answer that, tell me where it is going to be done and who is going to pay for it.
>
> *Joe Moss*

Right now a billion dollars of the taxpayers' money has gone into setting up treatment facilities for addicts all over the country. The goal of this administration is to get every addict into treatment.

Mark L. Cohen

We have addicts in my jurisdiction, but they are handled by churches and other voluntary organizations. We do not send them there; they go themselves. *Joe Moss*

When you look at the population of treatment facilities, you find that a high percentage of the patients are there because a judge or policeman told them to help themselves or go to jail. They may have been on probation after having been convicted of a minor crime and may have been told that if they did not stay in the treatment program their probation would be revoked.

So, ostensibly we have the same situation as that which exists in the Soviet Union where only three per cent of the people are involuntarily committed. Ninety-seven per cent are there voluntarily, but, if they do not stay put, within five seconds the hammer comes down and they are in involuntarily. That is the reason why the marihuana commission will propose a uniform bill providing for involuntary commitment petitions. The argument is that they will never be used, that they are just there in case someone steps out of line. The number of persons really in treatment voluntarily is an open question. *Mark L. Cohen*

The commission report does not come down in favor of mandatory minimals. But in considering the case for treatment, the fact is that it is a pretrial diversion, and perhaps other methods will be necessary. We cannot brush the whole thing aside by redefining it as a nonproblem; it is a real problem. *Henry Brill*

Assuming, however, that we are going to decriminalize drug possession, is referral to treatment a better alternative than taking addicts who commit crimes and putting them in jail?

The question basically eliminates a very significant part of the problem if no one will be charged with possession or use of narcotics.

If, indeed, possession and use are not criminal offenses, and if that undercuts the illegal market in drugs, then we will only be faced with persons who commit crimes and are, incidentally, addicts. Those persons should be put in prison. In the District of Columbia, for instance, if a person needs a psychiatrist he can get one more easily at Lorton, which is a correctional institution, than at St. Elizabeth's, which is a mental institution.   *Nicholas Kittrie*

The possibility of decriminalizing drug possession is about as likely as waking up tomorrow morning and finding the internal combustion engine banned. It just is not going to happen. We cannot look at decriminalization as a realistic possibility. But, assuming, hypothetically, that we are going to have decriminalization, do we prefer to see drug users who commit crimes locked up in jail or do we prefer to see them referred to a treatment program?

We no longer imprison individuals for addiction. That has been prohibited by the United States Supreme Court.
Joe Moss

Persons are not locked up for addiction, but for drug possession, a symptom of addiction, which is still a crime. We take a symptom of the disease and use that as a vehicle for locking up addicts.   *Mark L. Cohen*

This gets back to the age-old question regarding the extent to which one man should impress his views upon other men. We should go after drugs at their source, that is, where they are grown, and a secondary line of attack should be directed to places of importation. We only arrest addicts in Texas when they commit crimes other than addiction. If we find that an arrested person is an addict, we have no choice but to prosecute him as if he were not an addict. Once he is in custody, it becomes a problem for the medical authorities of the institution in which he is confined.

At one point we had a good program, where an addict could voluntarily go to a federal institution like the ones in Fort Worth or Lexington, and stay there X months or days, or for whatever period the local medical authorities thought was best for him. He would not be tried unless he refused to go. The program worked for a while but, regretfully, the Supreme Court banned it.[18] Making possession rather than addiction the crime is only playing with legal semantics since, obviously, addicts have drugs in their possession.   *Joe Moss*

If an individual can choose between treatment and prison, don't you have to make sure that the option does not really impose greater restrictions on the individual than if he were simply sentenced and sent to prison?

Only fifteen to twenty per cent of those convicted of crimes can be sent to prison because we do not have sufficient prison space. The people who get diverted into treatment are those who would otherwise be out on probation, so we are really looking at compulsory treatment versus probation, not compulsory treatment versus incarceration.   *Mark L. Cohen*

Involuntary treatment is a contradiction of terms. The favorite indoor sport of mankind is to persecute people. The only question is who to persecute. We have run out of blacks, women, and Jews, so we now persecute patients. We rotate the titles. A few years ago it was homosexuals and schizo-

18. Robinson v. California, 370 U.S. 660 (1962).

phrenics, but fashions change and now they are addicts. Five years from now it will be someone else. We talk about involuntary treatment as though we were dealing with a disease, but the two most rampant, objective, identifiable, and contagious diseases in America today have no legal compulsion behind them for treatment. You can have all the syphilis you want in New York City and no one can make you a victim because of it, but syphilis is a more objective and identifiable disease than addiction. Talking about involuntary treatment for addiction is on a par with another commission proposing a new treatment for addiction to coffee. If they decide that there is a coffee-addiction problem because the government does not like coffee, there will be a program of maintenance on tea. It is nonsensical.

Maintenance on methadone for addiction to heroin is like maintenance on scotch for addiction to bourbon. Although it is also ideological and political, it is essentially a business matter. Take it away from the private mafia and give it to the government mafia, the Special Action Office. It is a struggle for monopoly just as was the Opium War. Now we have methadone wars—conversion from heroin to methadone.

Thomas Szasz

One of the things happening now under the guise of trying to get people into treatment is that persons arrested for crimes are given a urinalysis to determine whether they are using drugs. This will not demonstrate whether a given person is an addict, but the judge will have an indication that he has used certain drugs. No lawyer is present at that time, and there is nothing to keep the judge from deciding that, because the individual is a drug user, he is going to keep him locked up by setting high bail.

The other alternative is to release the arrestee to a treatment program where he will be addicted to methadone. He may have tried drugs only two or three times, but the treatment program personnel can decide that, because he has had drugs in his urine, he has to be in the program and has to be addicted to methadone. They can require him to undergo continuing analysis, and then at the time of trial there will be no right for him either to escape prosecution or escape incarceration. So, there is a possibility that a person will be maintained on methadone up until the time of trial and then be sent to a state prison where he will be forced to undergo withdrawal.

That is the picture as it may evolve, and it is not farfetched. It is less farfetched than to believe that there will be any real public debate about drug decriminalization. *Mark L. Cohen*

Anyone who knows the technical side of methadone maintenance knows that it just cannot happen that way. An individual has to have a true history of heroin dependence, not merely a single specimen in the urine, before he will be placed in a maintenance program. Of course, there are physical indications—fresh needle marks and tracks—which also help to determine whether an individual is really dependent on heroin.

If an individual is transferred to methadone and then is convicted—withdrawal from methadone is the standard way to withdraw anyone from heroin. People talk about the horrors of withdrawal from methadone without realizing that it is the standard medical procedure for withdrawal from heroin in the Western World today. *Henry Brill*

There is controversy as to whether withdrawal from methadone is more traumatic than withdrawal from heroin. It takes a longer period. *Mark L. Cohen*

For the past fifteen years the standard method for withdrawal from heroin has been the use of methadone—long before it was used for maintenance.   *Henry Brill*

I supervise narcotic agents and my experience has shown that those on methadone do not regress to criminal activity. We have a recidivism rate in California of under five per cent.

The effects of withdrawing from methadone are by far greater than from heroin. In California we have not had one death from heroin withdrawal in the last ten years, whereas we have had many from methadone. Your statistics are wrong. Believe it or not, the average narcotic addict would like to lead a straight life; he would like to be able to buy a six-pack of beer, go to the drive-in, get up at eight and work until five o'clock in the afternoon. He does not want to stay in the cyclical pattern of heroin addiction; yet, the federal government has deemed it sufficient to allocate 150 slots for methadone maintenance programs to Los Angeles County when we have a waiting list of 3,400. Even though methadone is not the answer to the heroin problem, it is a step in the right direction.

We can talk about decriminalization, but it is not going to happen. The climate in the United States right now is not one which will permit the decriminalization of pot, much less heroin. Therefore, are we not faced with the necessity for treatment? It is disturbing when someone equates treatment with a form of genocide.

Of course, it is the same as the difference between winning a war and losing it. If the Germans had won they would have continued to call what they were doing treatment, which is what they called it all along; but they lost and, therefore, we called it genocide.

No one walks into a methadone maintenance clinic. The very language is misleading. If there were a free-market in drugs—

methadone, heroin, opium, methaqualone, and all the others —people could walk into a clinic as they now walk into a Ford dealership rather than a Chevrolet dealership. What we now have is people walking in under compulsion, and the entire semantics of protection have to be corrected. What we call treatment in America is ninety-nine per cent coercion. All involuntary mental treatment is harmful.   *Thomas Szasz*

Isn't it significant that in Los Angeles there is a waiting list free for people to sign up on—not a coercive waiting list? They want to get in and get off the heroin cycle.

They would not be on that list if they could go out and legally buy heroin. You say that is not a reality of life. It was not a reality of life to be Jewish in Germany, either. America was a very good country before 1914. People from all over the world were trying to come here. You could buy all the opium freely at a drugstore. Opium has been around for 5,000 years. It is the oldest drug known to mankind. Yet, we are now saying no one can live with it.

Hermann Goering was a chronic morphine addict. He was perfectly healthy and piloted airplanes. He never took methadone; I do not even know if methadone had been invented then. He had a choice among drugs, took morphine, and stayed perfectly well.   *Thomas Szasz*

To what extent should I be able to do what I please with my own body?

It is obvious that there can be no such thing as society without some consensus of what is permissible behavior. The way to determine this is by criminal sanctions. However, criminal sanctions are not synonomous with brutality; a $10 fine can be sufficient. An extremely difficult pharmacological technology is often needed to determine whether someone is taking a drug. If someone is clever, you will have a difficult time guessing he is on drugs. Freud was a cocaine addict for three and a half years. Halsted, the founder of the Johns Hopkins Medical School, was a lifetime morphine addict. About fifteen per cent of all the doctors in the Wehrmacht were on morphine for the fifteen years between World War I and the time Hitler remedied the situation.

You always hear about the models—the legal model, the medical model, and the sociological model. They are all wrong. Someone else teaches a model—religion.

My model is clearly a religion, reflecting Voltaire's philosophy. If you want to drink coffee, fine; if you want to take opium, all right; just leave me alone. This is essentially the ethic of individual freedom and the high respect for the common good, much higher than we now have.

Thomas Szasz

An individual probably should have control over his body, rather than the state, but I am not really sure the question concerning this was cast in the proper light because of the persons about whom we are talking. Part of the problem with the persons described is that they are jobless and underprivileged.

You assume that drugs cause irreparable damage to the body, but it is not clear what damage is caused by marihuana or heroin if used by persons who have the proper means, diet, and jobs.

There is evidence that some doctors taking drugs under controlled conditions, eating well, and sleeping properly are dying, but so what? They are taking a certain risk, not much worse than the risk taken when skydiving. The main thing about the persons you described and the reason for concern about them, is that they do not have a place to sleep nor do they have a proper diet.   *Nicholas Kittrie*

If there is a theoretically acceptable level of drug addiction in society, assume that eight to ten million is the acceptable number. If all those people are the ones without jobs, education, or the proper diet, such as people in the black community, are we willing to tolerate the addiction if it is only symptomatic, and not the cause of their state? Even if addiction exacerbates the problem, are we willing to go along with a system which enables this number of persons to get involved in drugs?

The number of persons who are opposed to drug dissemination and who are in favor of mandatory minimals is higher in the black community than it is among good, "right-thinking liberals" who have only studied the problem and had intellectual discussions about it.   *Mark L. Cohen*

Where do you doctors get your standards and how do you define a proper way of life? It is disturbing to have a few persons in a centralized place dictating how people should live and what a particular policy should be on detoxification or on any other treatment.

It is the judge, not the psychiatrist, who certifies a patient to a hospital or other treatment facility. Your point, then, is one you should take up with the judiciary.   *Henry Brill*

All the available money gets funneled into drug and alcohol programs. It is not spent to deal with many of the other social and economic problems that have plagued society for a long time and

that, in themselves, have had an effect on the use of drugs and alcohol.

Concerning the involuntary or voluntary commitment of drug addicts to mental institutions or to hospitals for detoxification as opposed to commitment to specialized treatment centers, it appears that what that does is make the hospital or the institution, and the doctor in charge of the patient, an alternative to prison and, thereby, makes the criminalization easier for the medical profession to accept.

Finally, there seems to be confusion about what drug addiction is. How can a medical doctor and a psychiatrist say that addiction is not a medical disease and that heroin or barbiturate withdrawal cannot cause physiological effects on the body?

> Of course, a person who is chronically taking heroin or methadone is in a physiologically different state from someone else, but the concept of disease has become like the concept of treatment, a very complicated philosophical and political concept which involves much more than a physiological or biological deviation from some norm. My own book, *The Myth of Mental Illness,* which was published some fifteen years ago, deals with this problem.

> The concept of disease involves at least two things: (1) a deviation from some norm which traditionally is a biological norm (in that sense, of course, baldness is a disease; syphilis, cancer, etc., have to be deviations from a bodily anatomical, physiological norm); and (2) in sociological jargon, the patient role.

> The patient role can come about in two diametrically opposite ways with diametrically opposite results. We have both voluntary and involuntary patients. They are called by the same name in America—patient—but they have nothing in

common. The difference between them is the same as the difference between someone who goes to West Point because he wants to become a soldier, and a draftee.

The patient role also involves the concept of a right to reject it. Is the Christian Scientist with cancer a patient? No, and if a doctor lays a hand on him, he is liable. I would have no objection to anyone calling addiction a disease, although I do not think it is, if the doctor who touches that patient against his will is just as liable as he would be with the Christian Scientist. Of course, the heroin addict is in a different state. That is why methadone maintenance sponsored by the government is a crime. It is the imposition of a disease. It is bad enough if you do it to yourself.   *Thomas Szasz*

Chapter 7

Marihuana

While marihuana was once claimed to be the cause of everything from insanity to murder, today, professionals and lay persons are having second thoughts. The change in attitude is evidenced more frequently in legislative proposals as well as social protest.

There is still substantial debate, however, concerning the use and legalization of marihuana, but the Bureau of Narcotics and Dangerous Drugs, for instance, now devotes little time and manpower to the problem. Proponents who argue for revision of the laws point out that twenty-six million Americans have tried marihuana and millions use it regularly. Public opinion will ultimately dictate the course of the legislative process.

The Authors

Richard D. Atkins
Marihuana Reconsidered

Mr. Atkins is an attorney in Philadelphia whose practice is largely devoted to representing persons accused of drug-related crimes. A graduate of the University of Pennsylvania Law School, he has written and lectured extensively on the problems of drug abuse and the law. Mr. Atkins was instrumental in revising Pennsylvania's drug laws and was appointed by Governor Milton Shapp as legal counsel to the Governor's Council on Drug and Alcohol Abuse in June 1972.

Lester Grinspoon
Marihuana: Yesterday and Today

Dr. Grinspoon serves as associate clinical professor of psychiatry at Harvard Medical School. He graduated from Tufts College and received his M.D. from Harvard Medical School. He also serves as director of psychiatry (research) at Massachusetts Mental Health Center. Dr. Grinspoon has lectured and written extensively, and is the author of *Marihuana Reconsidered* and *Schizophrenia: Pharmacotherapy and Psychotherapy.*

John Finlator
Federal Action and Inaction

Mr. Finlator is a consultant on drug problems to industry, educational institutions, and community action programs. Before entry into private practice he served as deputy director of the Bureau of Narcotics and Dangerous Drugs; he also served as director of the Bureau of Drug Abuse Control of the Food and Drug Administration, and was the director of Manpower and Administration of the General Services Administration.

R. Keith Stroup
A Time for Change

Mr. Stroup is the director of the National Organization for the Reform of Marihuana Laws (NORML). He founded NORML as a nonprofit, public interest lobby to re-educate the public about marihuana and its effects on those who use it. Mr. Stroup obtained his B.A. from the University of Illinois and his J.D. from Georgetown Law Center.

Marihuana Reconsidered

RICHARD D. ATKINS

An article, *"Marihuana, Assassin of Youth,"* by Harry J. Anslinger, the U.S. commissioner of narcotics, appeared in the February 1938 edition of *Reader's Digest.*

Mr. Anslinger described all the persons who had killed their
mothers, fathers, and others while under the influence of marihuana; the mother who complained about her daughter's death as
a result of marihuana addiction; and how people will crawl on the
floor and bark like a dog, etc., all as a result of marihuana use.

Attitudes

Even more unbelievable was a book from the late 1930s called *On the Trail of Marihuana, the Weed of Madness,* by Earle and
Robert Rowell, two opponents of liquor and cigarettes, who had,
at that time, turned their attention to marihuana. They published
what was then considered by many to be the latest authority on
marihuana. In the book they said:

> We now know that marihuana (1) destroyes the willpower, making a
> jellyfish of the user—he cannot say no; (2) eliminates the line between
> right and wrong and substitutes one's own worst desires or the base
> suggestions of others as the standard of right. Above all, it leads to
> crime and fills the victim with an irrepressible urge to violence. It
> incites him to revolting immorality, including rape and murder, and
> finally it causes insanity as a speciality.

> We saw that the subject in the earlier stages of marihuana use could be
> compared to a coiled rattlesnake, something that may turn dangerous in
> a split second. In the latter stages, he is completely a madman on the
> loose. Actually, he is temporarily insane. Although there are no real
> brain lesions as in insanity, there is an artificial insanity which in all
> other characteristics resembles the manifestations of genuine insanity.
> The marihuana addict may run amuck and wreak havoc. There is
> absolutely no predicting the results but of one thing you can be sure:
> He is not a safe person to be near under such a condition.

> "Kill, kill," cries the native of Malay as he dashes down the street with
> a dagger in his hands, maddened by hashish. Under its influence, the
> crazed user develops the urge to kill just for the sake of killing. Destruc-
> tion is the keynote and homicide the polestar guiding him in his mania-

cal acts. There is born a sadistic lust to kill for murder's own sake. Marihuana is rightly called the killer drug.

That was the attitude in the mid-1930s.

Legal Reform

House committees in Pennsylvania started working toward a full revision of the laws about three and a half years ago. Some persons recommended that marihuana should be legalized, but others did not; one woman even called the attorney general and said that she thought the death penalty should be imposed on persons who were arrested on marihuana charges. What was most remarkable and frightening was that the woman did not care if the person had a trial—mere arrest was enough.

Faced with such pressures from all sides, the House first came up with one bill, then the Senate, and then the Conference Committee. There were many proposals that were considered, with the final result that the possession of a "small" amount of marihuana was unanimously declared a misdemeanor with a maximum of thirty days imprisonment, whether it involved first or second or multiple arrests. That was a significant change from the prior five-year maximum. The legislators realized that in college and high school settings, most users of marihuana occasionally distribute it to friends or that one person may purchase it one time and another the next. Since that casual delivery, without remuneration, was the equivalent of possession, the thirty-day penalty was also applied to possession with intent to deliver a small amount, and for delivery of a small amount without remuneration. That contrasts with the previous penalty which was twenty years for the first offense and mandatory life for a third offense.

The legislature then considered the quantity that should be considered a "small" amount. It had to be an amount which would be appropriate for the entire state, and while it was felt that in Philadelphia three to six ounces, or even half a pound might be considered "small," some of the representatives felt that in other areas of the state, one or two joints would be a "small" amount. It was finally determined that approximately an ounce would be a proper amount to consider "small" throughout the Commonwealth. Some questioned what would happen if someone unwillingly purchased an ounce and got a gram or so more. The legislature, therefore, declared that instead of 28.375 grams as the limit of a "small" amount, the limit should be set at thirty grams to protect the purchaser. Similarly, when it was determined, after listening to all the evidence, that hashish was approximately three to five times as potent and approximately four times as expensive, a quarter of an ounce was set as the "small" amount limit for it. Instead of setting that limit at 7.205 grams, it was set at eight grams—again to protect someone who might purchase slightly more than the true "small" amount.

Another area of concern was the position marihuana should occupy on the schedule of controlled drugs. The original bills gave the Drug, Device and Cosmetics Board and the Secretary of Health the power, once a drug was scheduled, to reschedule it from the higher, more tightly controlled schedules or to remove the penalties entirely—remove it from control, based on the scientific and other evidence. The members of the House decided that was inappropriate and the power of removal from complete control was retained by the legislature. The compromise finally reached on all substances was that they can be changed from schedule to schedule by the secretary and the board, but that all penalties and all control can be removed only by the legislature.

Whether marihuana will ever be legalized in this state or elsewhere will not depend that much on chemical and scientific studies as to its harmfulness. It was clear that, in 1972 in Pennsylvania, it was public opinion that demanded that marihuana possession be reduced to a misdemeanor. The legislators received a great deal of pressure from their constituents because sons, daughters, and friends were getting involved.

A few years from now, if the legislature reconsiders, and if all the tests show that marihuana is relatively benign and very safe, even in its long-term effect, if the majority of the people at that time think that it should not be legalized, it will not be legalized. If in a few years there are studies which show that marihuana is very dangerous, but the majority of people are smoking it or are sympathetic to its use, then it will become legal. The legislative process is partly political, partly social, and certainly not all scientific.

Marihuana: Yesterday and Today

LESTER GRINSPOON

There now appears to be little doubt that among the commonly used psychoactive drugs, the amphetamines have a formidable potential for harm, psychological, physical, and social. It is clear that while they may be used, particularly in small doses over limited periods, without creating dependency, their use imposes the risk of severe dependency on many, and outright addiction on some. Animal data indicate that their chronic high-dose use may lead to cell damage in several organs, including the brain. In humans, chronic high-dose use often leads to short- and sometimes long-term psychoses. Even brief episodic exposure to moderate to high doses involves a significant degree of risk with respect to some physical disorders (e.g., cerebral hemorrhage) and psychoses. Furthermore, while it has not been conclusively established, there is a high degree of suspicion that prolonged high-dose use may lead, in some, to a global deterioration of mental functioning. There is, however, no doubt that the amphetamine abuser is more likely to become involved in destructive, often violent and impulsive, antisocial behavior.

Mirror-Image Relationship

There is a curious, albeit not perfect, mirror-image relationship between some aspects of cannabis and the amphetamines. Marihuana is not an addicting drug, and there are no serious sequelae upon cessation of chronic use; speed is addicting, and there is a withdrawal syndrome which often includes severe depression. While there is no convincing evidence that cannabis damages tissue, amphetamines appear to have that capacity; while there are no well-documented cases of death from marihuana, it is becoming increasingly clear that speed can indeed kill. Pot is not criminogenic and, in fact, being high on this drug probably diminishes the likelihood that a person may become engaged in violence and crime; just the opposite is the case with amphetamines. Cannabis in very large (usually ingested) doses is capable of producing toxic psychoses and in smaller smoked doses may rarely precipitate functional psychoses in individuals who are already vulnerable to psychoses, that is, persons whose psychoses might be precipitated by such events as an alcoholic debauch, an automobile accident, a surgical procedure, or a severe loss. It has been demonstrated that a psychosis which is all but indistinguishable from a schizophrenic reaction can be induced with amphetamines in "normal" subjects in the laboratory and paranoid reactions are not uncommon among speed freaks on the street. Speed quite clearly leads to the use of other psychoactive drugs; cannabis does not.

This is not to say that cannabis is a harmless drug; quite obviously it is not. Some persons experience adverse reactions, and some of the factors which seem to play a part in that are individual susceptibility, dose (particularly high doses of ingested cannabis), and unfavorable set and settings. However, the risk involved in using marihuana, excluding those which derive from its legal status, are of a different magnitude from those which arise from the psychopharmacological properties of amphetamines. In fact, the widely believed, largely mythological dangers of cannabis comprise a shoe which more nearly fits the amphetamines. Yet, the astonishing fact is that there has been an enormous concern and near hysterical outcry over the use of marihuana, while attitudes—public, governmental, and medical—toward the use of amphetamines have generally ranged from actual enthusiasm to complacency and, only recently, to some degree of concern.

Medicinal Use

To understand how attitudes toward those two classes of psychoactive agents became so divergent and so divorced from their actual relative potentials for harm, it is instructive to review some aspects of what may be referred to as the social histories of those two drugs. Cannabis has an ancient history as a medicinal agent; its first recorded use is to be found in the *Herbal,* an ancient equivalent of the United States *Pharmacopoeia,* written about 400 to 500 B.C. (It is often, and probably erroneously, dated at 2737 B.C.) But its entry into Western medicine occurred in 1830 when W. B. O'Shaughnessy, a thirty-year-old assistant surgeon and professor of chemistry in the Medical College of Calcutta, reported on his experiments in treating patients with rabies, rheumatism, epilepsy, and tetanus with tincture of hemp. He found it to be an effective analgesic and to have impressive anticonvulsant and muscle-relaxing properties. Stimulated by O'Shaughnessy's report, a number of Western physicians proceeded to explore the clinical possibilities of cannabis, and, within the next few decades, scores of papers on the medical usefulness of cannabis were to be found in the medical literature. Before long, it was fairly widely used in the United States in the treatment of a variety of ailments, many of which were symptomatically benefited, particularly by its analgesic and soporific effects. Several major limitations on its usefulness were imposed by the facts that it was not soluble in water and, therefore, could not be given parenterally, and that cannabis indica (the alcoholic tincture of cannabis, the form in which it was dispensed as a medicine) was notoriously unstable and physicians, therefore, could never be certain of dose. Its use as an analgesic began to be superseded by the opiates which were being used increasingly in the United States in the second half of the nineteenth century. When the hypodermic syringe was introduced from England in 1856, that use was accelerated, for the water-soluble opiates could be conveniently administered parenterally with predictable and rapid relief of pain. In fact, their use for the relief of pain became so widespread during the Civil War that opiate addiction became known as the "soldier's disease." With the development of synthetic analgesics such as aspirin, and synthetic hypnotics such as chloral hydrate and barbiturates, physicians lost interest in cannabis indica for its analgesic and hypnotic properties, for it was far less stable and, primarily for that reason, less reliable than the synthetics. Thus, in the early decades of the twentieth century its use as a medicine declined rapidly and its death knell was sounded with the passage of the 1937 Marihuana Tax Act.[19]

Curiously, during the heyday of its use, in America, as a medicine, there was only a very narrow appreciation of the fact that cannabis could be used as an intoxicant. Those who were aware of this property were largely intellectual and literary-minded readers of those writers of the French Romantic movement who together comprised the mid-nineteenth century Le Club des Haschischins. The two most important, where cannabis is concerned, were Theophile Gautier and Charles Baudelaire. Their effusive accounts were very influential, even though Gautier was describing the toxic psychosis induced by the very large doses of hashish he ingested, and even though there is considerable question as to whether what Baudelaire wrote about as hashish experiences were not, in fact, more truly Thomas De Quincey-influenced accounts of the effects of chronic use of laudanum (a mixture of opium and alcohol) on his very fertile and highly imaginative

19. Act of Aug. 2, 1937, ch. 553, 50 Stat. 551.

mind. The American counterpart to these authors was Fitz Hugh Ludlow, whose book, *The Hasheesh Eater: Being Passages from the Life of a Pythagorean*, was published in 1857. While, as with Baudelaire, there is some question as to how uncontaminated with De Quincey the descriptions provided by Ludlow are, there can be no doubt that his book was a success and excited the interest of intellectuals, although apparently not to the point where large numbers of them were turning on with cannabis. One way in which Ludlow differed from his European colleagues was that while they generally used hashish as the source of the drug, his was generally obtained from his "friendly apothecary" in the form of "Tilden's Extract" or some other brand of cannabis indica.

The writings of Fitz Hugh Ludlow were distinctive in that they provided one of the few connections in the American public's mind (and a narrow segment of it at that) between cannabis the medicine and cannabis the intoxicant. Furthermore, to the extent that general knowledge of the relationship between the medicine and the euphoriant existed at all, it had all but vanished during the half century that passed before cannabis in a different form (what we now know as marihuana, grass, dope, pot—the dried leaves and flowering tops of the *Cannabis sativa* plant) began to come into this country from below the southern border.

The Reefer

A good deal of mystery surrounds the story of the "reefer's" debut in the United States. It is generally assumed that in the early decades of this century, the custom of smoking the weed in cigarette form traveled with groups of itinerant Mexican workers across the Texas border into the southwestern and southern states. In 1910 the reefer began attracting some slight attention in New Orleans. By 1926, according to R. P. Walton, who studied the problem "on location," the city was wet with the habit. Supplies of marihuana came occasionally from Texas and more often by boat from Havana, Tampico, and Vera Cruz. Using New Orleans as a distributing center for the intoxicant, enterprising sailors became traffickers. The dried plant leaves were shipped from New Orleans up the Mississippi to various river ports and thence cross-country to large cities. It is said that by 1930 there was not one major American city which did not have a few marihuana smokers among its ranks.

In its early American years the reefer did not cause a great deal of consternation. However, as it became more popular among Mexican-Americans and a favorite of blacks, particularly jazz musicians in urban centers, and awareness of this use among those minority groups became more widespread, marihuana use began to arouse concern. In Louisiana, the *New Orleans Item* pointed a critical finger at the "moota" and hostilely claimed that the habit seemed to be most widespread among groups of foreign extraction. Clearly, the early fury aroused by marihuana can largely be attributed to the fact that it was introduced by Spanish-speaking people and blacks and that it was, therefore, considered an alien and un-American drug which was a particularly dangerous and degenerate intoxicant. Reflections of this increasingly widespread attitude were occasionally to be found even in the medical literature. In 1931 the *New Orleans Medical and Surgical Journal* stated that:

> The debasing and baneful influence of hashish and opium is not restricted to individuals but has manifested itself in nations and races as well. The dominant race and most enlightened countries are alcoholic, whilst the races and nations addicted to hemp and opium, some of which once attained to heights of culture and civilization, have deteriorated both mentally and physically.

In 1930, less than two years before the "benzedrine" inhaler first became available to the public, the Federal Bureau of Narcotics was founded. The bureau, under the leadership of its first director, H. J. Anslinger, undertook an "educational program" which must be some sort of landmark for its success in converting the general lack of concern with and ignorance about marihuana to widespread alarm and misinformation. In the year of the bureau's founding, only sixteen states had laws prohibiting the use of marihuana. By 1937, the year it succeeded in getting Congress to adopt the Marihuana Tax Act,[20] nearly every state had adopted legislation outlawing marihuana. The lay press, with the help of the bureau, contributed to the campaign with its frequent publication of alarmist stories of violent behavior, usually of a sexual nature, which, they asserted, all but invariably resulted from use of the weed. By 1950 the bureau, which had theretofore denied that the use of marihuana led to the use of opiates, embraced the so-called "stepping-stone hypothesis" which was to become the major argument against liberalization of the marihuana laws. A number of articles appeared in the early 1950s in support of that contention. The authors of the articles offered no supporting data; apparently they realized that the mass media audience had been sufficiently propagandized to accept the "stepping-stone" theory as self-evident. Had they presented what little data was available— for example, the rise in cannabis use was simultaneous with a leveling off or even a declining rate of opiate addiction over the preceding twenty years—they would have done little to support their claims.

Changing Attitudes

At about the same time, the American Medical Association was undergoing a remarkable shift in attitude toward cannabis. Before the passage of the 1937 Marihuana Tax Act, the American medical establishment had been quite interested in, and knowledgeable about, cannabis as a medicine, and had been sensible about its capacity for abuse. The change in attitude was symbolized by the fact that the only seriously dissident voice heard during the hearings before the House Ways and Means Committee which preceded passage of the act was that of Dr. W. C. Woodward, legislative counsel for the American Medical Association. While

20. *Ibid.*

he acknowledged a limited medical use for cannabis, he attempted to persuade the congressmen to initiate less restrictive legislation because of the possibility "that future investigators may show that there are substantial uses for cannabis." Dr. Woodward then went on to attack the evidence proffered by the Treasury Department on the "marihuana problem," particularly the claim that it was addicting, that it led to crime, and that its use was widespread among children. With the completion of his initial statement, Dr. Woodward was questioned by the committee in a most hostile fashion concerning his educational background, his relationship to the American Medical Association, and his views on the medical legislation of the previous fifteen years. Mr. Dingell chided Dr. Woodward: "The medical profession should be doing its utmost to aid in the suppression of this curse that is eating the very vitals of the Nation. . . . Are you not simply piqued because you were not consulted in the drafting of the bill?" Dr. Woodward was told that he was trying to throw obstacles in the federal government's way and, of course, none of his testimony was harkened to.

The House hearings were concluded without any substantial changes in the proposed bill, and the Senate hearings were conducted in a similar way. The bill became law on October 1, 1937, and, in its wake, many state laws, just as punitive and hastily conceived, were legislated. While its clinical use was already declining somewhat in the earlier part of this century, primarily because of the introduction of synthetic hypnotics and analgesics, the difficulties imposed on its use by the Marihuana Tax Act completed the medical demise of cannabis, and it was removed from the *United States Pharmacopoeia* and *National Formulary* in 1941. While, as previously mentioned, there had never been much of a public consciousness of the relationship between cannabis, the medicine, and marihuana, the weedlike intoxicant that blacks and Spanish-speaking persons used, the dropping of cannabis from the listings of legitimate medicines set the stage for the ignorance of doctors and for the change in their attitudes toward cannabis over the next thirty years. In protesting the impending 1937 Marihuana

Tax Act legislation, members of the Committee of Legislative Activities of the American Medical Association wrote: "Cannabis at the present time is slightly used for medicinal purposes, but it would seem worthwhile to maintain its status as a medicinal agent for such purposes as it now has. There is a possibility that a restudy of the drug by modern means may show other advantages to be derived from its medicinal use." Thirty years later a *Journal of the American Medical Association* position paper, written by men who have apparently had little, if any, experience with the use of cannabis drugs and apparently as little familiarity with the medical literature asserted: "Cannabis (marihuana) *has no known use in medical practice in most countries* of the world, including the United States."

This remarkable transformation of attitude toward cannabis is illustrated in the changing editorial policy of the American Medical Association. In September 1942 the *American Journal of Psychiatry* published a paper by Drs. S. Allentuck and K. M. Bowman entitled "The Psychiatric Aspects of Marihuana Intoxication" in which they asserted, among other things, that habituation to cannabis is not as strong as to tobacco or alcohol. Their report grew out of the studies they had carried out under the auspices of the La Guardia committee. In December 1942 the *Journal of the American Medical Association* subsequently published a reasoned, informative editorial on their work which was described as "a careful study." In reviewing the major findings of the study, the editorial proceeded to mention some possible therapeutic uses that might be made of the drug's properties. Those mentioned were the treatment of depression, the treatment of loss of appetite, and the possible treatment of addicts to opiate derivatives. However, following the *Journal's* publication of letters from H. J. Anslinger (January 1943) and R. J. Bouquet, expert on the Narcotics Commission of the League of Nations (April 1944), both of which denounced the La Guardia Report, the American Medical Association made an extraordinary about-face and joined the Federal Bureau of Narcotics in the denunciation of the report.

The switch was heralded by an editorial which appeared in the *Journal of the American Medical Association* in April 1945:

> For many years medical scientists have considered cannabis a dangerous drug. Nevertheless, a book called *Marihuana Problems* by the New York City Mayor's Committee on Marihuana submits an analysis by seventeen doctors of tests on seventy-seven prisoners and, on this narrow and thoroughly unscientific foundation, draws sweeping and inadequate conclusions which minimize the harmfulness of marihuana. Already the book has done harm. . . . The book states unqualifiedly to the public that the use of this narcotic does not lead to physical, mental or moral degeneration and that permanent deleterious effects from its continued use were not observed on seventy-seven prisoners. This statement has already done great damage to the cause of law enforcement. Public officials will do well to disregard this unscientific, uncritical study, and continue to regard marihuana as a menace wherever it is purveyed.

With this editorial the *Journal of the American Medical Association,* in the words of A. S. deRopp, "abandoned its customary restraint and voiced its editorial wrath in scolding tones. So fierce was the editorial that one might suppose that the learned members of the mayor's committee . . . had formed some unhallowed league with the 'tea-pad' proprietors to undermine the city's health by deliberately misrepresenting the facts about marihuana."

Over the past twenty-five years, the American Medical Association has been steadfast in maintaining a position on marihuana closely allied to that of the Federal Bureau of Narcotics. A great deal of misinformation and fear-generating mythology has come to surround this drug, and, judging by the published statements of the American Medical Association's Council on Mental Health, the medical community has been both a victim and an agent of this unfortunate process. This position is reflected in the editorial policy of the *Journal of the American Medical Association* which apparently disregards as "unscientific" and "uncritical" any study that does not demonstrate marihuana to be "a menace wherever it is purveyed." Thus the *Journal* has over recent years, with respect to cannabis, departed from the policy of accepting papers solely on the basis of criteria of medical importance and scientific soundness; clearly, it has consistently accepted papers, ones which from a scientific point of view have been of questionable worth but which tend to confirm the American Medical Association's view of marihuana as a great menace, and rejected those, regardless of scientific merit, which presented data and results which contradicted this view.

Thus, the medical establishment's view of cannabis has over the course of little more than a century come full turn. The same drug that had excited physicians' interest in 1839 and had become a respected and much used therapeutic tool during the remaining decades of the nineteenth century had increasingly, from the 1940s on, come to be regarded by American medicine with the same bias, fear, and ignorance as by the Federal Bureau of Narcotics. By the 1960s the American Medical Association had completely denied the medical heritage and potential of cannabis and its only interest in it appeared to be in providing quasi-scientific underpinnings to some of the now widely held myths.

Amphetamines

Amphetamine, on the other hand, came into being as a medicine and has for most of its short history enjoyed the unequivocal enthusiasm of the pharmaceutical industry and the medical profession. Only in the past several years has the medical establishment begun to be concerned about the consequences of its romance with the amphetamines.

In 1887 German pharmacologist L. Edeleano first synthesized the drug which would eventually become famous as "benzedrine," but he was uninterested in exploring its pharmacological properties and put this extraordinary stimulant back on the shelf. Not until 1910 did G. Barger and Sir H. H. Dale investigate the effects on experimental animals of this and a series of closely related chemical compounds, which they called "sympathomimetic amines." However, no one in America or England grasped the implications of their findings for another seventeen years, when Gordon Alles who was looking for a synthetic amine substitute for ephedrine concluded that the most effective of such substitutes was the original amphetamine synthesized by Edeleano. Because of his willingness to use himself as a human guinea pig, Alles not only discovered, very quickly, that amphetamine was active whether inhaled or taken orally, but also found that "benzedrine" was surpassed by its dextro isomer (later known as dexedrine) in its ability to alleviate fatigue, increase or intensify his alertness, and make him feel euphorically confident even when it kept him awake long into the night.

When F. P. Nabenhauer, the chief chemist at the drug house of Smith, Kline & French, found out about Alles' work he began to experiment with various commercial applications of amphetamine in conjunction with his firm's patented inhaling device. Realizing what a potential bonanza this "new" class of synthetic "ephedrine substitute" represented, the executives at Smith, Kline & French persuaded Alles to sell them all his patent rights, and in 1932 their "benzedrine" inhaler was first made available to the public by nonprescription, over-the-counter sales in drug stores across the country. The American Medical Association issued a mild parenthetical warning note in which it cautioned that "continued overdosage" might cause "restlessness and sleeplessness," but, at the same time, assured physicians that "no serious reactions have been observed." In late 1937 the American Medical Association approved the new drug in tablet form, recognizing it as an acceptable therapeutic medication for the treatment of narcolepsy and postencephalitic parkinsonism. The American Medical Association further stated that "benzedrine" was "useful" in the treatment of "certain depressive psychopathic conditions," and even that persons "under the strict supervision of a physician" could take amphetamine to capture "a sense of increased energy or capacity for work, or a feeling of exhilaration."

Complementing the enthusiastic overprescribing of amphetamines by physicians is the fact that since the 1930s there have been ways in which the public could procure these euphoriants with little or no assistance or interference from organized medicine, the Food and Drug Administration, or any state or federal drug-abuse control authorities. First, of course, there were the inhalers. Although Smith, Kline & French held the patent on the "benzedrine" inhaler until 1950, other drug companies quickly realized that they could sell their own imitations without fear of patent-infringement suit, because "benzedrine" was only one of an almost unlimited variety of equally stimulating, euphorigenic, and toxic amphetamine congeners. By the end of World War II, there were at least seven different inhalers on the market containing large amounts of those drugs, and all of them could be purchased at drug or grocery stores without a prescription. All of those products were very easy to break open, and the number of different techniques of ingestion was limited only by the ingenuity of the abusers. Although dissolving the fillers in alcohol or coffee produced the desired effects, a much stronger kick could be obtained by chewing these bits of cotton, or simply swallowing them whole.

While the inhalers introduced millions of young people to the amphetamines, most users found that it was just as easy to procure the pills. In the first three years after "benzedrine" was introduced in tablet form, sales rose to over fifty million units. The outbreak of World War II gave perhaps the greatest impetus to date to both the legal, medically authorized use and the illegal, black-market abuse of these drugs. When German Panzer troops invaded Poland, obliterated Warsaw, and turned west to rush through Belgium and France, they were taking large doses of methamphetamine to eliminate fatigue and maintain physical endurance. But the German army was by no means the only large-scale consumer of amphetamines during World War II; Japanese warriors and factory workers used as much or more. Nor was use of those stimulants limited to the Axis powers. According to British War statistics, seventy-two million standard dose amphetamine tablets were distributed to the British Armed Forces alone. Although the United States Armed Forces did not authorize the issue of amphetamines on a regular basis until the Korean conflict, "benzedrine" was used extensively by Army Air Corps personnel stationed in England, and it was an open secret that many pilots were engaged in a mammoth bootlegging operation. Amphetamines were also easily obtainable from military medical officers and aides. If only ten per cent of the American fighting men ever used amphetamines during that war, over 1.5 million men returned to this country in 1945 with some first-hand knowledge of the effects of these drugs. Indeed, in recent years the armed forces have constituted a veritable breeding ground for the abuse of all kinds of drugs, especially the amphetamines.

In recent years, amphetamine prescriptions have accounted for between six to ten per cent of all prescriptions for *any* drugs, including nonpharmaceuticals like penicillin, and a group of researchers in California have recently reported that at least one out of every five adults *admits* to long-term or habitual use of amphetamines. By 1946 Smith, Kline & French had been so successful in its amphetamine promotion campaign that a paper by W. R. Bett listed thirty-nine generally accepted "clinical uses" for the drug, including treatments of schizophrenia, morphine and codeine addictions, "nicotinism" (tobacco smoking), heart block, head injuries, infantile cerebral palsy, irradiation sickness, and hypotension. Bett, who further recommended the drug for ailments like seasickness, persistent hiccup, and even "caffeine mania," was only one of a huge number of physicians who regarded amphetamines as "versatile remedies" which were second only to a few other extraordinary drugs like aspirin in terms of the scope, efficacy, and safety of their effects.

Today, even though the Food and Drug Administration officially recognizes only "short-term appetite reduction," narcolepsy, some types of parkinsonism, and certain "behavioral" disorders in hyperkinetic young children as valid "therapeutic indications" for the amphetamines, the federal agency has no real power to limit the drug industry's advertising claims, and amphetamines continue to be prescribed by many physicians for nearly as many different reasons as Bett mentioned.

By 1958 the annual legal United States production of amphetamines had risen to 75,000 pounds, or 3.5 billion tablets—enough to supply every man, woman, and child with about twenty standard (5 mg) doses. Less than ten years later, the drug industry admitted it was pouring out 160,000 pounds, about 8 billion, amphetamine tablets per year, or enough for thirty-five to fifty pills for every living American. By 1970 reported legal amphetamine production had risen to over 10 billion tablets and in 1971 it rose again to over 12 billion.

While the national media, particularly in the late 1930s and early 1940s, were giving amphetamine a tremendous amount of publicity, even referring to the new drug as "poisonous," this did nothing to discourage use. Quite to the contrary, the numerous references to these "brain, pep, and superman" pills in popular press "news" stories and feature articles, even when ostensibly phrased as warnings, acted mainly to arouse the curiosity and interest of the American people. But the most important factor was the quick and amazingly enthusiastic reception accorded these inhalers and pills by the medical profession. The American Medical Association was especially influential in reinforcing the general impression that this was indeed a new wonder drug.

Public attitudes toward the amphetamines were initially, and for many years, either positive, neutral, or merely humorous, and the persons who used them did not, in the tremendous majority of cases, fit into any traditional stereotypes of "dope fiends." As long as the medical community was willing to accept the manufacturers' claims, no one was going to question why in 1932 practically any new psychoactive "medicine" could be marketed without any proof of either safety or efficacy. Nor did the American Medical Association, the Food and Drug Administration, or the Federal Bureau of Narcotics have any legal or sublegal authority to deny a drug company the right to sell practically any chemical not specificially forbidden by the Harrison Act of 1914.[21] All the Food and Drug Administration could do was recommend appropriate therapeutic indications; it had absolutely no power to limit or warn against consumer purchasing of drugs for which prescriptions were not required. Furthermore, the amphetamines clearly demonstrated the ease with which drug manufacturers could expand claims for their products and advertise their usefulness in an unlimited range of areas. Some drug firms obtained patents for their amphetamine congeners and combinations on the basis of these drugs' alleged "antidepressant" actions, and then expanded their advertising claims to include the "treatment" of conditions as disparate as obesity, alcoholism, enuresis, and so on; others took different tacks, starting from the claim that their product was "uniquely effective" in the treatment of obesity, but employing the same basic tactics.

Myths

Thus, in the mid-1930s, while marihuana was beginning to be brought to the public's attention through vilification, as a menace capable of wreaking great havoc, amphetamine was introduced and then promoted as perhaps the earliest technology-derived exemplar of better living through chemistry. Marihuana, having long since lost what little public awareness it once had as a medicine, was now identified with Spanish-speaking and black people. In view of the widespread bigotry and the attitudes toward and beliefs about these minority peoples which then existed, the mythology which grew up around marihuana is not surprising. Perhaps through the unconscious process of displacement it became particularly easy for people to believe that the drug of the blacks

21. Act. of Dec. 17, 1914, ch. 1, § 1, 38 Stat. 785.

and the Spanish-speaking must have something to do with crime, violence, sexual excess, addiction, personality deterioration, amotivation, etc. By the same token, to the extent that this kind of bigotry is still a vital force in the United States today, we would expect that it would be difficult, despite the increasingly widespread dissemination of evidence to the contrary, for persons to give up these false beliefs; this certainly appears to be the case. On the other hand, there are some facets of amphetamines and their history which may have made it more difficult for people to perceive them as more harmful than they are generally thought to be. They are, after all, products of modern technology and like many other such products, this fact, at least until very recently among a growing number of consumer skeptics, lent them a certain degree of legitimacy. Furthermore, whenever one picks up a trade journal in a doctor's office, he sees impressive, multicolor advertisements for the many amphetamine congeners. Perhaps most important, the crucial link in the selling of this drug (with respect to "legitimate" distribution) is the physician. The drug companies do not direct their enormous advertising campaigns to the consumer, but, because the various amphetamines are prescription drugs, the doctors are the recipients of countless pieces of promotional mail, medical journals are peppered with advertisements, and there are even outright gifts. When the doctor recommends a drug, he confers on it a great deal of legitimacy—so much so that the psychoactive agents that doctors recommend are medicines, not "drugs." What is more, beyond the fact that he is a physician and, therefore, an expert on drugs, the doctor is a figure in whom people have great trust. A recent public survey conducted by psychologists at the University of Connecticut listed twenty major occupations and asked participants to rate each from the standpoint of truthfulness, competence, and altruism; physicians came out on top with clergymen second. (Car salesmen were rated last, just one place behind politicians who were nineteenth.) To the extent that the doctor has been an unwitting pusher of this drug, he has also been a most trusted one.

Cultural Factors

Finally, cultural factors also appear to play an important role in the perpetuation of the mirror-image relationship that exists with regard to general views, attitudes, and beliefs about cannabis and amphetamine. Societies and cultures have certain norms for acceptable behavior and performance and tend to sanction, for social use, those drugs whose psychopharmacological properties are in accord with those norms. Cannabis has been accepted for centuries among the Brahmins in India whose cultural background and religious teaching support introspection, meditation, and bodily passivity while eschewing the life of action and individual achievement. Clearly, this more introspective, meditative, non-aggressive stereotype associated with marihuana goes against the Western cultural mainstream, perhaps particularly in the United States. The West, with its emphasis on achievement, activity, efficiency, speed, and agressiveness finds amphetamine much more culturally compatible than cannabis. Beyond this very general way in which the psychopharmacological properties of amphetamine make it fit so neatly to the fast-moving American culture template, there are some specific societal values and goals whose achievement is commonly thought to be abetted through the use of this drug. Thus, the many Americans who have been propagandized into placing great value on being energetic, confident, vitally dynamic, and very thin are particularly susceptible to the lure of a drug with a grossly unappreciated potential for harm.

Federal Action
and Inaction

JOHN FINLATOR

  Marihuana Reconsidered, by Dr. Lester Grinspoon, is a scholarly work which discusses the medical side of marihuana. A companion piece is *Marihuana, the New Prohibition,* by John Kaplan, professor of law at Stanford University. From both legal and medical points of view, these are two of the most outstanding works available.

Professor Kaplan studied members of the football team at Stanford University and their drug use. He found that seventy-three per cent of the football team that beat Ohio State in the Rose Bowl three or four years ago had used marihuana at one time or another. As a matter of fact, he found there was more marihuana use by members of the first team than by those who sat on the bench, but he did not know what the correlation was between the two.

The Bureau

Most of you know the problems that the Federal Bureau of Narcotics and Dangerous Drugs has had, and the stance that it took. Most of it was born in ignorance. The bureau did what it did because the medical profession and the scientific community let it happen. It was a wide open field—they grabbed the ball and ran with it.

We all know the story and history of marihuana, but even at the hearings on the Tax Act, [22] Congressman Snell asked what the bill was about and Sam Rayburn said that it had something to do with something called marihuana, which he believed was a narcotic of some kind.

At that time, Harry Anslinger had become commissioner of Narcotics and had already made his stamp on the world. He "bulled" through the stories about marihuana. They were not all his fault. The administration itself actually pushed the horrors of marihuana. Harry Anslinger was the man with the charisma, the personality, the ringmaster, the clown. He was the one who could speak, and speak he did; he just overwhelmed the House and the Senate on every bill that considered marihuana, and in nice, sweet, docile compliance they did what he said. The scientific world

22. Marihuana Tax Act, Act of Aug. 2, 1937, ch. 553, 50 Stat. 551.

never spoke up, nor did the medical or legal professions, with the exception of Dr. W. C. Woodward, who went to Washington and was berated because Harry Anslinger passed the word, "Kill him." That was the kind of man we had running the bureau at that time.

Alcohol

Marihuana, however, is not really our worst problem. Our worst problem is something that the president's commission has just told us about—alcohol. Dr. Joel Fort, who is on the program, has a new book called *Alcohol, America's Biggest Drug Problem.* But alcohol does not bother us anymore, although it should. We have settled that one. We have gone through alcohol prohibition and no one really gives a damn about that problem anymore.

Legislation

The first national legislation to regulate narcotic distribution was the Act of 1909,[23] which was an act that prohibited the importation and use of opium. It was very ineffective. There was no way to enforce it. It just floundered around and nothing happened.

In 1914 we became even more concerned about the narcotic problem and passed the Harrison Act.[24] It provided for fines up to $2,000 and five years in jail, but was unenforceable, although they tried to enforce it with the Narcotic Division, which was in the Prohibition Unit of what was then the IRS.

By 1930, though, we had severed that little unit and created something called the Federal Bureau of Narcotics. That was when the hard push against marihuana began. Actually, the effort was not all at the federal level. At one time thirty-one states had laws against marihuana before there was any federal law concerning it.

23. Act. of Feb. 9, 1909, ch. 100, 35 Stat. 614.
24. Act of Dec. 17, 1914, ch. 1, § 1, 38 Stat. 785.

Some of the reasons for the drive against marihuana have been explained—racial prejudice and the fear that it was addicting. The stories that came out of the Geneva Convention of 1925 had their effects on the states, but it was the bureau that took up the cudgel and really made marihuana the "killer" weed. When those words were coming from our federal government they became important; it was out of the mouth of the Great White Father—when he said something, people believed it. As a matter of fact, close to eighty per cent of the people believe it right now.

The Narcotics Control Act of 1956[25] imposed stronger penalty structures on narcotics and included marihuana within its coverage. Again, there was no opposition from the medical profession, the scientific world, nor the legal profession. It just rolled through.

Then, in the 1960s, marihuana became the thing. The bureau still fought hard against it, but something else happened—the law enforcement bureau of the Food and Drug Administration, HEW, called the Bureau of Drug Abuse Control (BDAC) was established. We took a rather soft line on marihuana. We did not think that it was that bad, and we realized that there were many other things that were much worse. However, in 1968, we amalgamated the old FBN and BDAC and put them into the President's Bureau of Narcotics and Dangerous Drugs. The merger resulted in a change of attitude. In one of the bureaus we had a chief medical officer, and we had a staff of pharmacologists and scientists. They had an effect upon the new bureau, so by the time we got past the Controlled Substances Act of 1970,[26] the bureau itself had proposed lessening the penalties on first-time marihuana offenses. That was not enough for many persons but the proposal did come from a law enforcement bureau—something which may have been considered strange by many persons.

25. Narcotics Control Act of 1956, ch. 629, 70 Stat. 567.
26. 21 U.S.C. § 801 (1970).

So, today we see that the bureau has changed to the extent that it spends very little time or manpower on the marihuana problem. The bureau is still officially against it and the laws are still against it, but a real metamorphosis has taken place.

A Time
for Change

R. KEITH STROUP
It is important to understand that the marihuana issue is not, in fact, a smoker's issue. At the National Organization for the Reform of Marihuana Laws (NORML) we spend a lot of time trying to impress that on people. The fact is that persons in this country now smoke marihuana in great numbers as a matter of personal choice. We in the panel today have pretty well established that the laws are wrong. They originated in prejudice and ignorance, but we still have them, and they exist on the federal level. There are twenty-six million Americans who have smoked marihuana at least once and there are thirteen million who consider themselves regular smokers. That means that sixteen per cent of the adult population in this country break the law. Sixty-seven per cent of all college students have smoked marihuana—that is two out of three. There are 280,000 retail "dealers" in this country, all of whom are outlaws. They import approximately four tons of marihuana every day. An estimated thirteen per cent of it is confiscated and eighty-seven per cent gets through to the consumer.

Arrests

It is estimated that there were 226,000 marihuana-related arrests in this country last year, over a quarter of a million, and yet, we hear the police tell us confidently that the emphasis is no longer on marihuana. The police often tell us that they are only after the pusher, not the user, yet the statistics do not back that up. Of those 226,000 arrests, most of which were on a state level, ninety-three per cent were for possession and use, while only seven per cent were for sale. Of those arrests that were for possession and use, two-thirds were for possession of less than one ounce—hardly what would be considered a big dealer.

The state of Texas still has a law that permits from two years to life in prison for simple possession of even the smallest amount of marihuana. In Texas right now there are over seven hundred persons locked up for possession and use of marihuana, with the average length of sentence nine and one-half years. If you think about that, you will agree that it is incredibly shocking. Those persons have done nothing that most of you have not done, that I have not done, and that fifteen per cent of our adult population does not do now; but they were caught and, more than that, they were caught in the wrong place.

Federal Response

We are trying to get the government to understand that once there is a significant, although minority, portion of the population that is determined to use a drug like marihuana as a recreational drug, and once it has been established that marihuana does not present any significant threat to the society as a whole, or to the individual user, the government's role should be the same as it is with other "legal" drugs—to minimize the potential for abuse. That is really what we should be talking about. The government's role is not to lock up persons who differ in their choice of drugs, whether they choose alcohol or marihuana.

Age

The government's role should be to minimize the potential for abuse, and there are two areas in which it can contribute to that. One is the age area. There is no doubt that a lot of persons thirteen, fourteen, and fifteen years old get marihuana and smoke it. Even those who have come out strongly in favor of legalizing marihuana agree that there is a potential for hazard that we should not permit. The Canadian Commission, which was the equivalent of our National Commission on Marihuana and Drug Abuse, recommended in its report the decriminalization of marihuana in Canada and indicated that the only area of concern they had was adolescent use and abuse. It is not that marihuana is particularly harmful to the adolescent who occasionally gets it; it is rather that the adolescent does not necessarily have the maturity to know when or to what extent to use it, and may end up basing his life on marihuana or other drugs and may not develop his coping mechanisms. The only way you can control that sort of problem is through a regulatory system, some form of government regulation over the distribution which would require that a person be a certain age, probably eighteen, before he could get it.

We know the "alcohol age" doesn't work perfectly. Most of us managed to get alcohol before we were eighteen or twenty-one. However, such regulation does have the effect of creating a policy of social discouragement. Most older Americans do not understand that it is more difficult today for adolescents to get alcohol than it is for them to get marihuana.

Adulteration

The second area in which the government can validly act to curb the potential for abuse is with adulteration. While it may not yet be a major problem—and I hope it does not develop into one—there are indications that some marihuana grown, say in Kansas, may not be very strong and sometimes is adulterated with much more potentially harmful drugs such as the hallucinogens, acid NBA, and strychnine. The person who has decided to smoke marihuana should not have to take the added risk of not knowing what has been added to it. Clearly, the government should realize that it is not in its interest to have a marihuana consumer playing a grab-bag game. When you buy marihuana, testing it before you buy it by smoking a joint, your decision to buy is, assumedly, based on whether you think it is good, whether you get high from smoking the joint. The consumer has no way of knowing whether he is getting high from good marihuana, or whether it is weak marihuana that has had LSD added to it. The government must understand that we are only going to be able to control adulteration and will only have an impact on adolescent drug use by having some system of distribution other than the black-market.

However, that would mean some form of legalization, and legalization, in the public's mind, has numerous bad connotations. It means no control and often means commercialization, although it does not necessarily have to result in either. Legalization does not mean that the cigarette companies will automatically enter the market and make millions of dollars. The point is that, at this time, we need to minimize the areas in which the potential for abuse is greatest.

Proposals

It would be impossible to read the proposals which President Nixon recently made concerning drugs, including mandatory life sentences, selective use of the death penalty, and a general over-all reliance on the deterrent effect of criminal penalties to combat all unwanted drug use without thinking back to the drug legislation passed in the 1930s. In particular, the president's willingness to ignore the many excellent studies which have been made available to him, including the results of the National Commission on Marihuana and Drug Abuse, and to cling to his long-standing reliance on the criminal approach for use and even possession of marihuana, is reminiscent of the 1930s.

If the Congress and the state legislatures were to consider marihuana prohibition today, with no prior history of emotionalism and prejudice, not a single one would prohibit its use with criminal sanctions. Most would probably discourage its use, regulate its distribution and sale, control purity to avoid problems of adulteration, and add a tax as a means of raising needed revenue. Those were precisely the recommendations of the new comprehensive report by the Consumers Union in *Licit and Illicit Drugs.*

Today, we seem to be at a social impasse. Everyone is willing to say we were wrong in the 1930s, that we overestimated marihuana's potential for harm, and that we probably legislated out of ignorance. Yet, marihuana prohibition continues out of a general fear that public misinformation and morality are rooted so deeply as to spell political defeat for anyone who would challenge it.

NORML

At NORML we perceive our job as principally twofold. On one hand, we spend as much time as possible with legislators and their staffs in an attempt to be sure that they are well informed about marihuana and its potential effects on the user. We want to be sure that whatever stand they take, albeit shaped by the politics of reality, is an informed stand.

On the other hand, a major portion of our work has to do with public re-education. We must demonstrate to the elected officials that significant segments of the population have changed their minds about marihuana prohibition and are now willing to experiment with a noncriminal approach. In a country as big as this, that necessarily requires the involvement of opinion makers, both individually and institutionally. It is obviously impossible to discuss the issues personally with over 200 million people. We are all busy and all have a myriad of issues fighting for our attention.

Policies

For most persons, the marihuana laws simply do not merit high enough priority to permit firsthand investigation, so they look for signposts, for indications that they can use to form their personal positions. That is where you can be of great help.

As Dr. Grinspoon documented in his book, *Marihuana Reconsidered,* the American Medical Association (AMA) has been particularly at fault in the continuation of an ill-advised drug policy in this country. After its lonely opposition to the earlier legislative efforts, the AMA quickly fell in line, and up to the present time has supported the status quo. It appears that its interest in the marihuana issue has been limited to the periodic publication of articles purporting to show the harmful effects of its use. Last year, after the governing board of the AMA recommended a policy which would have endorsed the recommendations of the National Commission on Marihuana and Drug Abuse, the AMA House of Delegates refused to adopt it. They backed off, opting instead for a statement in vague terms which seemed to approve the use of misdemeanor penalties.

A misdemeanor in this country permits one year in jail and/or a $1,000 fine. If you have any idea of the conditions of our jails and of the natural consequences of spending a year locked up, you will understand that that is no light penalty. Certainly, it is progress, better than life imprisonment, which is still the maximum permissible sentence for possession of marihuana in Texas, but the person who goes to jail in this country, even for a year, may find the truly dangerous drugs more available there than on the street. He will likely be subjected to homosexual attack, and will surely leave his prison experience with considerable alienation and bitterness for the system which unfairly defined him as a criminal. For what reason? What has he done that is so harmful that we cage him like an animal? Whom are we helping by making him a criminal? Obviously, we are only exacerbating the situation. The medical evidence is so conclusive on the side of decriminalization and the evils of unnecessary criminalizing people so obvious that the AMA can no longer refuse to act.

The same applies to the American Bar Association (ABA). It appears that 1972 was the first year that the ABA has ever taken a stand of any kind concerning marihuana prohibition. Since most legislators are lawyers, it is incredible that the ABA has chosen to ignore the issue so long. Despite the recommendations of two separate committees that the ABA endorse decriminalization, the House of Delegates, like the AMA, backed off at its convention. Apparently not wanting to appear to be acting in haste, they offered a resolution that condemned excessive penalties but clearly left open the possibility of misdemeanor sanctions.

Our government has a policy of discouraging all recreational drug use. That includes alcohol, tobacco, and marihuana. We concur in this policy and we are willing to work hand in hand with the government toward that goal. But the campaign should be honest, it should be factual, and it should avoid the mythology of the 1930s. Most importantly, it should altogether avoid the use of criminal penalties for those who, despite our advice to the contrary, continue to smoke marihuana.

Change

We must continue research into the potential ill effects of long-term marihuana use. If there is anything harmful about marihuana, certainly we smokers want to know. We should warn the consumer of the potential harm, as we now do with cigarettes, but, while we are warning, we should stop making criminals out of those who simply ignore our advice.

There is still much debate about how we should handle legal marihuana, whether it should be available through liquor stores, whether private companies should be allowed to sell it, what type of government controls should be imposed, etc. Of course, there is a need for more study in many of those areas, but, in the meantime, let us stop focusing our law enforcement efforts on the users. Twenty-six million Americans have now tried marihuana, including two-thirds of the nation's college students; thirteen million use it regularly—it is time we changed the laws.

Discussion

What is NORML doing in terms of influencing public opinion, especially with regard to the media?

There is a prejudice in the media against legalization because of the control of older persons who went through thirty-five years of indoctrination and who are frightened by it. We find that numerous times persons are afraid to allow us to present our views because they assume that we are screaming radicals who will wreak havoc on their program. What we try to do to offset that impression is to explain that the issue has very little, if anything, to do with smoking marihuana; it has to do with man's freedom. We are generally finding that there is a second reaction. The media is fascinated by the subject of marihuana and there are times when we have been allowed to explain the process in which we are involved. There are times that the issue may be given more media play than it deserves because of that fascination.

I know it may surprise you, but the truth is that state legislators are not generally ignorant about marihuana. They have staffs, they read books, and they know now that marihuana does not present a significant threat. But it is not an issue like Vietnam and they are not going to make or break their careers over the marihuana law. So, while privately, both in Washington and on the state level, they will assure you that they understand and would be delighted if they could remove criminal penalties altogether, the fact is that until we can demonstrate to them that such a stand will not throw them out of office, most will not have the courage to act. Jacob Javits and Harold Hughes, on the federal level, are obvious exceptions.

The manner in which public opinion will be best affected is by working through groups like the Jaycees. We have a group in Dallas, Texas, called Concerned Parents for Marihuana Reform. They represent parents of kids who have been arrested and some still have kids in jail. These are persons who are not generally involved in the political system. But when the suburban housewife goes down and talks to the Governor of Texas about her son who is locked up for twenty-three years in a Dallas jail, he listens, and much more so than he does to us.

Specifically, the answer to your media question is that we have not been able to bring suit against the FCC because we honestly do not feel that we have a case to make at this point. We did file a protest with the FCC when they covered something Nixon said about marihuana and we wanted equal time. They documented, convincingly to me, that marihuana had been given quite a bit of time on the evening news.

R. Keith Stroup

A recommendation to control methaqualone was submitted to the Bureau of Narcotics and Dangerous Drugs (BNDD). The process would take three to six months. It seems clear that the bureaucracy in Washington is extremely prone to pressures from the pharmaceutical industry. I wonder what is the procedure of study and why is it that when the dangers have been known for at least a year, there is still no pressure being applied to control the use, etc., of the drug.

The reasons are many. First, the government has to determine that the drug is abused. One cannot say so just because that is read in the news. The point must be proven. Once that is done, then a hearing must be held. The manufacturers can come in and object to any proposal. If they do, then the BNDD has to get the permission or advice of the secretary of

Health, Education, and Welfare (HEW), and sometimes it takes time for those two organizations to come to an agreement. When they do, the drug is placed on the schedule. Sometimes they can move pretty fast, and I think that they are going to move pretty fast on this one.

It is a long process. Each step has to be taken before the next one, and very often there are arguments between the scientific side of the government, HEW, and the enforcement side—the Justice Department.   *John Finlator*

What steps would you recommend for the regulation of drugs— how would you evaluate and regulate drugs in a wiser way?

That is an enormous question and one, of course, with which we are all struggling. As far as the American Medical Association (AMA) part of the problem is concerned, it has been remiss in its approach. The AMA has allowed itself to be used as an instrument to provide a kind of quasi-scientific rational for various attempts at moral hegemony. The literature on masturbation at the turn of this century, when there was a great moral concern about that "evil" practice, indicated that a person who masturbated would shrink his brain, would become demotivated, and would have sexual difficulties. Clearly, physicians allowed themselves to be used in a moral issue. Similarly, that has happened with regard to marihuana. There are other motivations for the AMA's approach to such other drugs as amphetamines.

Generally, there should be a total ban on the advertising of all drugs as one step toward a more rational approach to the use of drugs. We are providing a kind of drug "education" to everyone in this country which, unfortunately, is a kind of education in which we tell youngsters who watch the television (some surveys indicate that children watch television more hours than they go to school) and see pills go into a little plastic man, that their problems, whatever they may be, get solved through drugs.

There should be control and decriminalization of marihuana, legal availability with control, but we should certainly not allow the tobacco or alcohol industries to become involved.

Lester Grinspoon

We should not make it too easy for the government to put things under its control. We have too much control already. For example, most of you will remember the banana peel bit in 1966 or 1967 when we got stories from the West Coast that you could take a banana peel, scrape it, do certain things with it, smoke it, and you had a real high. The AP and UPI picked the story up, and it went all over the nation. The Bureau of Drug Abuse bought thirty pounds of bananas, brought them into the laboratory, cooked them, steamed them, and smoked them. We did everything we could to those things for about sixty days, trying to arrive at a real conclusion. When we finally came to the real conclusion, the put-on was all over. We put out a nice press release which no one picked up.

John Finlator

Chapter 8

Education

Drug information is big business in the United States. It has captured the attention of Congress, federal agencies, committees, and the public at large; yet, there is no evidence that this massive drug-abuse education effort has worked.

Information is vital to the success of any educational effort, but the misinformation problem has become so serious that the National Commission on Marihuana and Drug Abuse has recommended a moratorium on the production of new information materials. Critics of drug education programs insist that we should stop dealing with drug information anyway and begin focusing on human needs.

The Author

Peter G. Hammond
The Great Drug Education Game
Mr. Hammond is director of communications for the Special Action Office for Drug Abuse Prevention. Before assuming this position, he served as executive director of the National Coordinating Council on Drug Education, a private, nonprofit organization which has worked to promote rational approaches to all drug-related issues. Mr. Hammond is an author, lecturer, and drug education consultant to numerous organizations.

The Great Drug
Education Game

PETER G. HAMMOND

You have been burned. Half your mari-
huana turns out to be oregano; throw that half away or use it on
pizza and you lose half your stash. You get paranoid and flush five
lids down the john; that will cost you $25 for the roto-rooter man.
You inhale a still-burning joint while trying to get the last hit; go to
the freak clinic and pay $15. You are busted and must become an
agent informer to save your own miserable hide; use that card to
send the player of your choice to jail and you lose five ounces of
dope plus all your friends. That is from "Beds and Heads," a
monopoly-style game of "pot" luck which has not been taken too
seriously in drug education.

Junkie Game

But we have another game that is called the "Junkie Game."
The Junkie Game has been designed by the Haight-Ashbury Free
Medical Clinic in San Francisco to give people a realistic appreciation of the bleak life of heroin addicts. The game has been developed as a realistic educational tool, a training device for socially
relevant recreational experience. Two to seven players begin with a
job, $500 in cash, possessions, and pick up a heroin habit after
first throwing the dice. Other aspects of the game include wisdom
cards, hassle cards, hustle cards, and the center square—death—
which puts you out of the game. If you get back to the starting
point after a $20-a-day habit, you redeem your possessions, get
your job back, become clean for good, and you win.

The Junkie Game costs $9 and it is further evidence of one of
the phenomena which has become apparent during the past four
years in drug education—drug information has become very big
business in the United States. It has captured the imagination of
presidents, legislators, bureaucrats, school boards, publishers, film

producers, and gadget makers. It has moved drugs into first place in our health education programs and has occupied the energies of at least seven different congressional committees and thirteen federal government agencies. It has created commissions, task forces, councils, conferences at Villanova, and has made instant experts out of thousands of persons who never knew a thing about drug education. It has given a new lease on life to the export business. One of our "concerned film makers" has successfully sold over 2,000 prints of a drug education film at $250 each and, soon, with some dubbing, will make that same film available in French and Spanish.

Failure

There is only one thing that drug education has not done. It has not worked. There is no evidence that our massive drug-abuse education effort has worked. In fact, it has backfired on us and the full consequences have not yet been calculated. The National Education Association's year-long study on drug education in America reported these findings this past summer: (1) the greater percentage of existing drug education programs are superficially or educationally poor; (2) some of the programs, because of false statements made by misinformed or uninformed educators, could very well have contributed to the increase of drug usage in our society; (3) much money is being wasted on poor materials and misinformation; (4) the use of false, poor, emotionally oriented and judgmental material is much more harmful than no material at all.

The key to the drug education game is having information; you cannot play the game unless you have it. What the Coordinating Council has been doing for the past three years is evaluating some of the information. It discovered that, among other things, eighty-four per cent of existing drug-abuse education films contain scientific or medical misstatements about drugs and drug effects, and that one-third of them contain so many errors that they should be classified as scientifically unacceptable. After systematically reviewing more than 220 films, the council can barely recommend sixteen per cent of them. The errors range from misstatements of fact and misleading innuendoes, from inaccurate portrayals of the drugs and their effects, to distortions of scientific data. The only thing they seem to do very well is show the proper administration of illegal drugs. Over half of the films available for classroom instruction in the Philadelphia metropolitan area schools come from the list of scientifically unacceptable films.

Posters, charts, giveaways, throwaways, pamphlets, dial wheels, slide charts, and all the other general public drug education information literature is much worse than even the films. When our evaluation is complete at the end of this week, probably no more than ten pieces of literature should be recommended from over 300 separate items that litter the countryside.

The council updates, through monthly supplements, a loose-leaf reference notebook that covers twenty-six areas of drug information ranging from epidemiology to street drug analysis, from law enforcement to an underground drug digest, from alcohol to cannabis. This publication, *Grassroots,* operates under the assumption that one can trust most contemporary pieces of drug information to be valid and relevant almost as much as you can trust the drugs sold by your friendly street pusher to be potent, safe, and unadulterated.

The misinformation situation has become so serious and widespread in the United States that one of the recommendations of the National Commission on Marihuana and Drug Abuse called for a moratorium on the production of new information materials. By early April 1973, about ten to fifteen major national groups in the country, including the National Education Association and National Association of Secondary School Principals, will have joined the call for a moratorium on the production and distribution of drug education materials. Such a development will enable us to catch up on our evaluation and determine the kinds of new materials, if any, that may be necessary to rid ourselves of the existing misinformation.

Errors

As is usually the case when a big idea goes wrong in a very big way, there is a sequence of mistakes which must shoulder the blame for the failure. No one error, no one failure by itself, is at fault for the drug-abuse education catastrophe. We have identified the following as contributing factors: (1) failure to question our intentions and assumptions; (2) failure to define the problem correctly; (3) failure to establish realistic goals; (4) failure to evaluate the validity of our messages and messengers; and (5) probably most important, failure to correct our mistakes.

Today the great drug education game continues and is still being perpetuated through invalid assumptions that range from "drugs are a youth problem" to "adults know what is right"; from "only illegal drugs are misused" to "abstinence is the best goal"; from "facts can change behavior" to "unless you have tried them you cannot talk about them." We have focused our entire education effort on indiscriminate dissemination of the so-called facts. We have confused information with education. The role played by facts in determining use is unclear, and teaching facts as the basis for decision making assumes that we use them in that process. However, information levels have not been shown to play a dominant role among the factors related to the different forms of drug use. The presentation of "just the facts" might well lead persons to conclude that even powerful illicit substances produce pleasure and can be used with little risk.

We have clearly failed to understand the nature of the problem. We see certain drugs instead of certain issues; we see pat answers instead of probing questions; we see "them" instead of "us"; and we see a threat to our moral security instead of a challenge to our inventiveness. No one understands the drug problem well enough to try to solve it with education, and not enough persons understand education well enough to deal with drug abuse. We rush to the media with advertising slogans and jingles from wornout heroes, but we forget that while advertising can shift brand preferences and create new markets, what it can do to manipulate values is still unknown.

Operation Intercept produced some heroin addicts and some speed freaks when some pot became scarce. Our current experience with the national "turn-in-the-pusher" hotline has undermined the services of existing community hotline programs. The banning of TV advertising has been one of the factors that has increased the use of nicotine because of the use of other advertising gimmickry, and will, most probably, work the same result with drugs, if the foes of over-the-counter advertising have their way.

The list is endless, but the procedure is the same. Public hysteria fed by misinformation has pushed us to short-term action solutions and the well-publicized rush to act has too often only worsened the situation it was meant to correct. Drug education has to deal with all of these problems—after all, that is what education is all about—the sorting out, interpretation, and accommodation of the confusion that exists in the world. However, without realistic goals, the task is impossible. Abstinence cannot work until we outlaw curiosity or until persons are willing to learn vicariously. On the other hand, teaching persons how to use drugs is, at the present time, socially undesirable. The options available in between are much more realistic and functional, and present the new light for drug-use education and information.

New Efforts

Although there have been some shifts in the traditional information campaigns that we have witnessed over the past few years, most new efforts, as the result of an infusion of government funding, still depend too heavily on information about drugs. They have, however, begun, in some way, to incorporate drug-relevant issues and have attempted to focus on behavior and attitudes. Unfortunately, the trend is compartmentalized. It has been kept within drug education as it stands in the traditional health curriculum, rather than spreading out—discussing morphine addiction in history class, examining epidemiology in math class, tracing traffic routes in geography class, or analyzing the content of street drugs in chemistry class. The intransigence of school administrators and the rigidity of school curricula in general, coupled with the general failure of American educational institutions to provide relevance and meaning to the learning process, suggest the urgent need for a new setting for drug education.

The new kind of drug education should not neglect information about drugs, but should assume that information does not influence behavior until it is processed by an individual in terms of his own experiences, feelings, and lifestyle. More meaning should be placed on the functions of drug use rather than on psychological or physiological effects. The new approach should abandon charts, films, and ecstatic testimonials for rap sessions, role-playing, and alternative behavior, and should focus on the family as a unit.

With any new focus, we are going to need a new setting, and I would suggest something other than a structured classroom. The teacher should be a participant, the students should be participants, and the subject might from time to time be drugs. With a new setting, we are going to need some new billets, and these will necessarily vary from community to community, but the goals should be simple, uncomplicated, direct, and attainable— something like learning to listen or learning to express oneself. If we feel a compulsion to focus on drugs, cleaning out misinformation in the school or in the public library has some innovative merits.

For a community where experimentation is inevitable, we should probably focus on interpreting initial drug experiences. That is a critical point in the drug cycle with which neither education, treatment, nor law enforcement deals. All of our experiences and knowledge about drugs and drug effects are hidden from the experimenter. He is inevitably left to peer cheers and to other traditional attitudinal influences. He is not prepared or equipped to sort feeling from expectation or reality from anticipation. Yet, while his decision at that juncture will determine his drug behavior for years to come, we do not, now, bother to reach him because we have not yet bothered to create the mechanism.

Goals

One thing is clear—there is much we need to know about realistic drug education goals. We must stop dealing with drug information and focus on human needs. Our efforts to reduce the casualty rates from the misuse of drugs would be enhanced overnight if we could substitute what we think we know about drugs for what we do know about human behavior.

In time, our civilization will perish and our great-great-grandson, the archaeologist, will be digging in our ruins. Buried there along with computers, weapons, and the rest, will be found tons and tons of papers with words printed in all languages. Many of these words will be about drugs—words like modality, rap, cyclasazine, score, lid, bust, coordinate and hotline, needle, poison, O'Dale, BNDD, SADAP, LEAA, NIMH, ASA, conference, seminar, and law—and he will conclude that we were a people addicted to words. We were all word freaks. We got up every day, every hour, with more words. He will wonder at the strangeness of a people who could talk so much and do so little to help each other.

Discussion

I wonder about the availability of the information that you handle, and what it would cost. You mentioned *Grassroots*, which

I believe costs $96 a year. Is that not expensive for drug information?

No, it is inexpensive, if you look at the publication. It is a two-volume binder which contains twenty-six categories of information and is updated monthly. It is essentially our review and evaluation of all of the articles, reviews, and publications that appear on a regular basis, with some information services so that it is useful to you. It is published in cooperation with the Student Association for the Study of Hallucinogens (SASH) in Wisconsin. The American Bar Association and the American Medical Association are both members of our council. We have a newsletter, *The National Drug Reporter,* which comes out on a biweekly basis and contains most of the information found in *Grassroots* in capsule version. Subscription to that newsletter is $9.

You said half of the films used in Philadelphia area schools were found to be unacceptable. Were any of the other half in the recommended category?

We have essentially four categories of films. We have a recommended category and a restricted category within which are films that contain either conceptual inaccuracies or scientific misstatements that are not too serious. Most of the films in the Philadelphia area fall within that category as well as our third category, the scientifically unacceptable.

The final category of films includes those aimed at minority groups. Out of the 220 films that are available, only seven of them were made for black audiences, which gives you an idea where everyone's heads are. Interestingly enough, our review panel rejected all seven films as being very biased, very racist, and for perpetuating some incredibly invalid assumptions about drugs. It is always a black male; he is always using heroin; it is always Trashcan Alley; and there are no positive role models for the young people who view the film.

We publish a report called *Drug Abuse Films*. It is a comprehensive review of 220 films which also explains how to use them. One creative way to use films in medical schools is to show one of the unacceptable ones and ask the students to identify all the errors in it.

What about rap sessions and the drug education game that you mentioned?

I think the game is middle class. We are opting for and have tried, at least in the state of New Jersey, an en masse parade of ex-addicts before you, as part of the game. Have you ever seen an ugly ex-addict? He is usually a very tall, articulate, well-spoken individual who talks to people who have acne and Cs on their report cards and who just broke up with their best friends. He stands up in front of them saying, "Hey, drugs have ruined my life." There is really no evidence of that, and he probably gets $200 for the rap. If you put an ex-addict into a one-to-one situation, it does not take long for any student, middle class or otherwise, to cut through all the garbage he has been feeding him.

How does the government output compare with private industry?

The government effort is improving considerably. Dr. Jaffe, who heads the Special Action Office for Drug-Abuse Prevention, has at least made an attempt to avoid some of the conflicting information that has been characteristic of the government efforts during the past five to ten years of our epidemic of drug interest. The quality of information is improving. In terms of volume, it is not as high as that in the private sector. In terms of what drug companies are putting out, the information is in the mediocre category, but some effort and money have been put into telling you to stay away from certain kinds of drugs.

Chapter 9

Problems

What is drug abuse? That question is especially difficult to answer in a society that is taught to use drugs for every ache and pain. Use is so widespread and so completely a part of the American way of life that drug careerism may well be the biggest growth industry today.

It is doubtful that politicians and administrators will solve the many problems that exist; there are too many weaknesses in too many areas. Deeper understanding is desperately needed, but it is not being provided in the places where it is needed, such as the classroom and courts of law. Before we can achieve greater understanding, we will have to explore the social, institutional, and individual pathologies that underlie the drug-abuse problem.

The Authors

Joel Fort
Understanding the Drug Problem

Dr. Fort is the founder-leader of the National Center for Solving Special Social and Health Problems in San Francisco, a private, nonprofit, futuristic program providing comprehensive help for people of all backgrounds. He was previously a consultant to the World Health Organization on Drug-Abuse Problems, and is now a lecturer in criminology at the University of California

177

at Berkeley. He is the author of *The Pleasure Seekers: The Drug Crisis, Youth and Society* and *Alcohol: Our Biggest Drug Problem.*

Lisa A. Richette
Justice: A Matter of Courage

Judge Richette was appointed judge of the Philadelphia Court of Common Pleas in 1971. She is a graduate of the University of Pennsylvania and received her law degree from Yale University. She served as chief of the Family Court Division of the Philadelphia District Attorney's Office, and is the author of *The Throwaway Children.* Judge Richette has taught at the law schools of Yale, Pennsylvania, and Temple. She is featured in *Who's Who in America.*

Sidney H. Schnoll
Beware the Classroom

Dr. Schnoll is a National Institute of Mental Health Special Fellow in Neuropharmacology at Thomas Jefferson University in Philadelphia. He is the medical director of HELP, INC., a free clinic, which administers to many of the young people in the Philadelphia area. Dr. Schnoll has served as medical coordinator at many rock festivals, and is an author, lecturer, and consultant on the pharmacological, medical, and sociological aspects of drug abuse.

Understanding the Drug Problem

JOEL FORT

We talk glibly about drugs and the drug problem but seldom do we understand what we are talking about. The word "drug," as certainly all medical students know, includes everything from aspirin and penicillin to the mind-altering drugs which begin, not with marihuana, but with alcohol and tobacco, our most widely used and abused drugs. As good Americans, we deal with widespread, illegal possession of alcohol and tobacco by those under age through hypocrisy. We ignore the fact that it is happening and generally begin our discussions of the drug-abuse problem with consideration of the other more political and sensationalized mind-altering substances. The true psychoactive drug context ranges from A (alcohol) to H (heroin) and includes, of course, pot, acid, speed, and a host of other substances.

Drug Abuse

What is drug abuse? For some, it is any illegal use, including in that terribly inaccurate definition, alcohol and tobacco use by those under the age of eighteen or twenty-one. For others, it is use of a drug, of which they disapprove, by someone they do not like, particularly if that person does not visit barber shops regularly or work a traditional forty-hour week. But, actually, any drug can be used once or occasionally. Some use may be regular with only a segment of that abuse, meaning excessive use that damages health, social, or vocational functionings.

Some self-appointed expert will stand before a group—he has traditionally been the drug policeman or a politician—and drop the term "hard drugs" out of the side of his mouth. We react with a knee jerk, horror response, ready to march on our capitols and demand new criminal laws. Of course, that is, in part, because we crave oversimplified pseudosolutions in America, and the politicians, most of whom are lawyers, pander to that. They tell us that the solution is to pass a law or elect them to office. That concept of "hard drugs" has been embedded in our minds, and certainly in the minds of the older generation.

Both the John Birch Society and the Communist party would agree that death is a hard phenomenon. Any drug that is involved, significantly, in producing death or disability should be called "hard." Thus, we get to the million deaths produced each year by alcohol and tobacco and by a wide range of other drugs. Psychosis is another hard effect, and leads us to alcohol, amphetamines, LSD, occasionally marihuana, and occasionally other drugs.

Certainly we include addiction as a hard effect and that brings us not only to narcotics but to alcohol, and sedatives such as barbiturates, Doriden, Miltown, and Quaalude.

Motivation

People use drugs for many different reasons, but, basically, because drug use is institutionalized in our society. We are taught to use drugs for every pain, problem, or trouble. Fortunately, more people have joined in the condemnation of advertising of alcohol, tobacco, and pills. But advertising is not the only culprit. Beyond that there is the role-model example children are shown by adults as they grow up. We take for granted that when we relate to another human being the best way to deal with the situation is to hold a glass of alcohol in our hands, have either a dried tobacco plant or a dried plant we call marihuana in our mouth, or drop a pill. We seldom turn on to the warmth and character of another human being or feel that we can enjoy ourselves or deal with difficulty or tension without using a chemical. Doctors, of course, contribute to that by their massive overprescribing of drugs, as does the pharmaceutical industry by its massive overproduction.

Programs

Most federal and state drug problems are total failures, regardless of the image building that we hear from the speech-writers of the compliant political psychiatrists in the drug bureaucracy. A recent book described those who got us into the Vietnam War as the best and the brightest. If that was, indeed, the case, those who lead our federal and state drug efforts are frequently the worst and the dullest.

Operation Golden Flow—national urine testing—assembly line methadone maintenance programs, harsher penalties, and increased government control are measures our federal leaders tell us will solve the drug problem. The implication is that heroin addiction is the only drug problem, and that all we have to do is use this combination of urine and methadone, perhaps mixing them together, and we will solve not only the drug problem, but all the criminal problems in America.

One solution to such a situation would be to hold the persons who have been totally ineffective and detrimental accountable—accountability is lacking in our institutions. A step forward would be for such persons to resign.

Drug Careerism

The biggest growth industry in America today is drug careerism. There are probably more persons working in drug treatment, drug education, and drug research, and attending drug meetings than there are drug abusers in America. Although it perhaps does not exceed the gross national product of General Motors, it certainly is a growth industry in which some of you may well have stock.

Social Reaction

We are prisoners of mythologies; we are following outmoded traditions and rules. We have anachronistic organizations such as the American Medical Association (AMA) and the American Bar Association (ABA) supposedly guiding us, or testifying in our behalf, and, in the case of medical and law schools, we attend outmoded and obsolescent educational institutions.

Drugs have been overglamorized and oversensationalized on both their good and evil sides. Not everyone should use drugs and not all drugs are good—drugs such as alcohol, tobacco, pills, and marihuana. Rather, the expectations of good about all these drugs have been almost as exaggerated as the expectations of evil. Unfortunately, there is no drug, including alcohol or marihuana, that will make an ignoramus into a genius, solve school or family problems, or rebuild neighborhoods. One of the reasons for crusading for decriminalization of private drug use and for moving the society beyond drugs is that there is a reverse relationship between dealing with oppression, with injustice, and with every uncomfortable situation through a chemical on one hand, and attacking the roots of discontent in bringing about the long-overdue revitalization of our institutions on the other. So, let us try to evolve an independent position that gets away from the ridiculous polarities between those who advocate pot in every chicken, and those who call for the death penalty for the first offense and castration for the second.

Pleasure is desirable, and the Declaration of Independence guarantees us life, liberty, and the pursuit of happiness. But, as far as drugs are concerned, they are, at best, one of many sources of pleasure and meaning in life and their effect rests not on the magical property of the drug but on the personality, characteristic, and mood of the user. However, there are many other sources of pleasure and meaning in life, and one of the solutions to the many drug problems, therefore, is to provide a wide range of alternatives, including the practice of making medical and law schools mind-expanding experiences rather than ones which disillusion and make an increasing number of persons cynical.

Institutional Pollution

A core problem in America is "institutional pollution"—the bureaucratic-political-diplomatic process with its crises of mediocrity and senility. Congress is the best example, our largest and most expensive rest home in America, and the state legislatures are not far behind. Institutional pollution is one of the chief alienating factors in American society and no one can hope to understand drug use or abuse unless he recognizes that it is symptomatic or barometric of that pollution, and of affluence, poverty, racism, and a variety of other things present in American society. We attack only the branches. As Thoreau once said,

"There are a thousand people hacking away at the branches of evil for every one striking at the roots," and our leaders and our mass media keep us looking at those branches, keep us from understanding what the roots are, and, therefore, make the problem much worse.

We need to confront the new barbarians in our society. The least able are governing us as they did in ancient Rome. We need to stress the positive alternatives in social action. We need to demythologize drugs, and we need to become more and more aware that one person with courage can constitute a majority. We should not continue to ask the politicians, the bureaucrats, the administrators to solve these problems for us. We need a brick-by-brick rebuilding of our society which only you and I can accomplish.

Justice: A Matter of Courage

LISA A. RICHETTE

Jim Markham wrote an excellent article in the *New York Times,* "Heroin and Hunger May Not a Mugger Make," on the premise that you just do not explain crime by equating it with drug addiction. The problem of drug addiction is an outgrowth of many things that happen to people in very early years.

Judicial Response

It is all very well to say that we ought to decriminalize addiction, but what happens when you have someone in front of you who has been found guilty, either by you or by a jury, of having committed a felony, such as an armed robbery, and he is then ordered to have a presentence or a psychiatric report. Assume he is nineteen, twenty, or twenty-one years old, because that is the age of most of the persons who come before me. The report comes back and you find that you are faced with a person who has a severe addiction. My alternatives as a judge are: (1) to put the person on probation, which is an almost meaningless gesture because of the vast numbers of cases each probation officer has to handle; (2) to send him to a penitentiary where he is not going to get any kind of personal attention, either for his drug addiction or for anything else that happens to be wrong with his life; or (3) to place him in a therapeutic community that ostensibly is going to focus on the addiction but in the process of doing that will do a lot of other things in terms of changing the person's human value systems and orientation, and so forth.

That is the struggle a judge faces, inevitably propped up by psychiatric and probation reports that are valid. It takes a great deal of courage and integrity to do what you think is right.

Alternatives

What we need in our criminal justice system are the largest kinds of alternatives. There are some persons who are so troubled and who are so violent that they cannot be placed in one of the community-based drug programs. A district attorney once told a young man from Gaudenzia House that the program there was "neonazi" and that was the reason why he was not going to support a sentencing recommendation. To the contrary, it is not neonazi. It is a way of reaching people that is far less nazistic than what goes on in our state prisons. What we need are more secure hospital settings where persons who have these very special problems can go and get adequate therapy.

Basic Problems

The simplistic solutions to complicated human problems always mask an underlying antihumanity. Throughout history, those who have advocated simple and "ultimate" solutions have always been against man. Today, they focus on drugs, which are only a symbol of the kinds of boredom, misery, and despair that persons who never get near a law school or a medical school feel in this country—the people of the slums, the people of the ghettos. We have to focus on the social, institutional, and individual patholo- gies that underlie the drug problem. In other words, we have to get back to those old basics of poverty, racism, lost economic and educational opportunities, disintegrating families, and, above all, a collapsing criminal justice system. All of these problems seem to be very uninteresting to our national leaders. In fact, at the same time we hear severe, draconian penalties called for, we see a severe reduction in educational, social welfare, and other programs, on the grounds that they are inefficient. It is the same old problem; people have to understand that the solution does not lie in a voltage of electricity that passes through a human body but in a whole new way of how we look at people.

Comte Maurice Maeterlinck said, "For every person who would push humanity forward, there are a thousand who would hold it back." When there are only a few persons trying, in their own ineffectual and imperfect ways, to push humanity forward, it is too easy for the "politicization" process to continue and to make thousands of persons confused and disturbed about what is hap- pening. What we need are educated, courageous, and independent judges.

Beware the
Classroom

SIDNEY H. SCHNOLL
One of the prime things that is taught in medical and law schools is to emulate those who teach. Most of

the time that teachers are in classrooms is spent teaching students to be just as they are, to act the way they do, to look the way they do, and to uphold "the profession."

Failure

In one instance, when students completing medical school were asked what they had missed, the bulk of them replied that they would have preferred courses in how to set up a practice, medical liability, investment—all things which were important to managing their own personal lives but which had nothing to do with taking care of the persons a doctor is supposed to care for. Look at what doctors do in emergency rooms with persons who come in with an alcoholic problem. They are shoved into a corner, they are thrown to the side, they are looked down upon. That is what we are taught to emulate.

P.R.N.

If any of you ever have a chance to go to a hospital and look at some medical charts, you will see how physicians abdicate their responsibility. It is done very simply with three letters, P.R.N. That means that the nurse can administer a medication as she sees fit, and that the doctor is not to be interrupted, especially at night when he is sleeping. He does not want to know that his patient has a headache, cannot sleep, or is having a problem. If he does not want to know about it, why did he go into medicine? The drug companies have certainly taught us that there is a drug for every problem and the P.R.N. order is a solution. The most important thing you have to remember is: Do you want to be molded in their image or in your own?

Discussion

How do you handle the situation, in a juvenile case, of an individual who has been declared deprived and who may want to go home, but you have different and competing institutions trying to get hold of him?

> At Villanova Law School we sought to take third-year law students into Delaware County, where there were no legal services for juveniles, to represent them. All I could do then was to help each person to find a proper solution for himself. You must never equivocate and never accept the rhetoric of rehabilitation; never accept at face value what some probation officer or some psychiatrist says that that institution or this foster home is going to provide.
>
> What we did was to attempt to involve every juvenile in the decision about where he would go. We would take them out to an institution and have them walk around and talk to other persons there. If the court would not allow that child to get out of detention, we would be absolutely opposed and would take an appeal. Some of the students even went out and found alternatives to institutionalization. They went out and spent the time and effort to find foster homes for the kids.
>
> *Lisa A. Richette*

It seems that both doctors and lawyers are taught to be very paternalistic. If a patient is informed of what a drug does, why should he not be allowed to take it as needed—P.R.N.? Why must the doctor be informed about every headache in the middle of the night? Why should a patient not have the right to decide what his doctor knows about him, even if he is in a hospital?

Following that, what about persons who choose drugs as their alternative, as their meaningful experience? In some cases, they do not want to become vegetables, and in others they do. We should let them make a decision. After all, it is their life.

How many doctors tell their patients what the drugs do to them? In my school, the pharmacist tells the patient what the side effects are. How many do it in practice? Very, very few.

Of all the specialties in medicine, neurology is the one least associated with care of the patient. When you do find out he has a headache, do you see him every day? I question your right to accuse other doctors of being lax in daily care.

I am not going to try to defend neurology, because I do not think neurology is the greatest profession in the world. When I was talking about the P.R.N. use of medication by physicians, I was talking about its indiscriminate use. When I was in medical school, I was taught by the internist on the service that when I wrote orders, I should always include a P.R.N. order for a headache medication, a P.R.N. order for a sleep medication, and a P.R.N. order for a laxative. That is still being taught to many medical students in this country. It is indiscriminate use of the P.R.N. type of medication. The doctor does not know if the patient is constipated and even if he is, the constipation could be caused by a bowel cancer. The doctor should check, but he does not. The fact is that if you looked at the charts in almost any hospital you would find that some charts will have as many as twelve to thirteen P.R.N. medications on them. Now, certainly, there are some medications that can be given P.R.N., but I am talking about indiscriminate and excessive use. When that happens, the physician is abdicating his responsibility to find out what is wrong and help the patient.

Someone else brought up the point about the use of drugs to get high for an experience. I was not talking about that. I was talking about what we were trained to do in medical school, and that is something entirely different.

Physicians do abdicate their responsibilities to the patients; they avoid them, and give them as little time as possible. Giving a drug to someone who has a severe psychological problem means that the doctor does not have to deal with the problem; he can stay away from it.   *Sidney H. Schnoll*

How many doctors actually tell the patients what medication they are going to get and what it is going to do to them? None? Is that really another part of the paternalistic role that doctors are encouraged to play in medical school? They know what is right for the patient better than he does. Therefore, they do not explain what a drug is or what is wrong.

It is not so much paternalism as authoritarianism. To what extent can medicine, the law, and all the authoritarian control systems superimpose their own judgments on individual judgments? It is a very important philosophical question which is being raised and cannot be avoided. *Lisa A. Richette*

I see it as a much broader and somewhat different issue. How often does a lawyer explain to people the range of possibilities available to them in the system that we call administration of justice—the different dispositions, the plea bargaining, the adversary system, the deal making, the whole range? How often does a doctor explain to people the implications of methadone maintenance, of antabuse, or of psychoanalytic therapy? How often does the self-help program describe what is involved in the kind of commitment it expects people to make and the devices that are used as part of that? While it does involve authoritarianism, it is much more than maternal and paternal.

One other thing I wanted to discuss is that for us to get to medical school or law school, and for us to survive that process, requires a marked degree of overconformity. Our whole acculturation is geared to keep us under the control of the least able people, who learn how to manipulate us, how to use image building to replace reality, and how to divert us from the sources of our discontents.

We have to confront all of that, beginning where we are. For example, why is curriculum not shortened? Why do you need to spend four years in medical school or three years in law school? The reason why there were not more blacks, Puerto Ricans, and women at the drug-abuse symposium is not because the persons who planned the meeting did not want them; it is because your medical schools and law schools do not admit them.   *Joel Fort*

One major thing that is lacking in medical and law schools, which reflects on the education they offer, is responsible and receptive admissions policies. I speak as a veteran of seventeen medical school rejections, with a husband who has a record of twenty-six medical school rejections because he failed organic chemistry the first time, although he got an "A" the second time.

Sometimes, of course, rejection can be a good thing because it may force you to find something else. I found law. I found a dean who looked at my degree in chemistry and looked at my law school admissions test scores. They were looking for women and I was admitted. It was a good year for women.

The problem with the medical and the legal professions lies with the admissions committees. They get hung up on hair, and they get hung up on beards. The great emphasis on grades results in the admission of brilliant students who do not know how to talk to people and who care only about their grades. Their attitude carries over into their professional lives with the result that we end up with a lot of professionals, people who are supposed to treat the problems of others, who do not care about the people with whom they deal.

That is not going to change until the admissions criteria change. It does not take brilliant persons to be doctors; you do not have to be a chemist or a biochemist. It takes persons who care. Do we really have enough of them?

> I have been involved in the movement to humanize the legal profession and it is not easy because there is great resistance on the part of professors, degree holders, and chair holders who feel very threatened by the influx of a whole new philosophy. *Lisa A. Richette*

Are you aware that in our methadone program here in Philadelphia, there is no provision for rehabilitation; that the methadone maintenance program which was funded by the federal and state governments is aimed at recidivism?

> I have very strong views about methadone and they have been made very clear. I do not know about the current methadone maintenance program but I have had any number of persons who have come in accused of crime, who were on methadone maintenance and getting their methadone regularly. I am sure that they were not getting other therapy, because they told me so. *Lisa A. Richette*

We have gone to a great deal of effort trying to make sure that the persons who work in our programs are qualified. We try to train our counselors and social workers, but we never try to train the physician who has a very large impact on the program, or the psychiatrist who works in the program.

I have heard it said that the psychiatrists who work in methadone programs are usually persons who cannot make it in private practice, cannot make it in any of the state mental institutions and, therefore, wind up in methadone. I do not know if that is true of the psychiatrists, but I think it is true of some of the physicians who work in the programs part time and have no concept about the drug that they are administering. If we are going to have some effect, I think we should make a major effort to make sure that anyone who works in the rehabilitation or treatment of any of the addictive diseases knows what he is doing and is trained in the area of his so-called expertise.   *Sidney H. Schnoll*

Ninety-nine per cent of the persons working in drug treatment programs today, particularly methadone maintenance programs, had no contact with heroin addicts or any other drug abusers before the past two or three years. They are basically trained in traditional Freudian psychotherapy and its application to affluent, white, middle-class women who do not get well too quickly and never pay their bills. By simply renaming that method "community mental health," it has been made applicable to drug abuse, racial conflicts, poverty, sexuality, and a variety of other things. That is why our methadone programs and other so-called mental health programs do so poorly. We need to have staff people who know what they are doing. Most importantly, methadone should not be presented with the commitment that the recipient will eventually be able to get free of it as well as free of heroin. While we should have a rule that there have to be comprehensive services offered in addition to mere maintenance, we also must guard against putting more time, energy, and personnel into methadone than we do into the wide range of possible alternatives.

What we need lies not in our curriculum or our practices, but in something much more fundamental. We must work out ways to stop branding persons as criminals for their private behavior—sexual, drug, gambling, or whatever—and we must work out ways to prevent them from becoming ill in the first place. Even if medicine were far more effective than it is now, we should still be placing ninety per cent of our emphasis on prevention. Both of our systems, the so-called administration of justice and the so-called delivery of health services, are terribly inefficient. They need to be renovated with stress placed upon decriminalization and preventive medicine.   *Joel Fort*

How can a professional lawyer or physician avoid cynicism and believe that he could actually work to change things?

Oscar Wilde defined a cynic very well as one who knows the price of everything and the value of nothing. The first step toward social change is to be able to point out that the emperor has no clothes, and the second step is, then, to reclothe the emperor, not to be satisfied simply with pointing out the absurdity.

I do not know how one can completely avoid cynicism or pessimism; to attempt to explain that would be pseudo-scientific. The answer depends upon one's own life experiences and character. The national effort to change our whole approach to drug and sex problems has certainly made some impact. Change is not a result of any one person's effort, but one person can provide a foundation and, depending upon his energy level, and his initiative, he may be able to take his cause to millions of persons through radio, TV, and articles.

You can reach a vast number of persons. We err in thinking in all or nothing terms. If we ask, "How do I change the whole country by tomorrow morning?" we have set it up in such a way as to give ourselves a copout, an excuse for doing nothing.

The brick-by-brick concept means that we should start with our own families, our own agencies, our own schools, our own classes, the organizations of which we are a part, and we should try there to change outmoded procedures, confront abuses of authority, and make the institutions human and relevant to what is going on in society. We must find others who share our vision of what needs to be done, and then we gradually change it.

We can no longer expect Democrats, Republicans, liberals, conservatives, lectern-pounders like myself, my wife, or anyone else, to change the system. It has to be all of us and the sooner we realize it, the better off we will be. The process, even if we do not succeed, is what makes our lives meaningful.   *Joel Fort*

The only reason you can say you are a cynic is because you are a white male. You have never had to live in an oppressive situation. You have never really had to struggle for human acceptance. I have always been involved with persons who have been oppressed, and they are not cynical. Black persons in this country have an enormous amount of energy and they do not use it to rationalize their own inactivity. We need to work, constructively, even for a very small change-producing project, and to work with other people. Out of a joint effort comes a force that is greater than the individual component. Perhaps, apart from thinking of the dreariness and blackness of your educational process, you should set up your own educational systems. Who says that the only way you can learn how to be a lawyer is by ingesting what Villanova or the University of Pennsylvania Law Schools think you need to know? You must take responsibility for your own education, and you must get involved on every level with persons around you.   *Lisa A. Richette*

Students often hear the same cut-and-dried lectures. How can a subject be presented more specifically? We can talk generalizations, but where, specifically, can you really teach us how to deal with persons and what to do?

Persons that want to get involved are going to, but in a class of 200 there may only be about ten persons who get involved. The persons who have M.D.'s, those in a position to help in a methadone maintenance program, are not doing a thing. I want to know how we may generate the interest necessary to motivate them.

> There are two areas in which there is great natural interest, sex and drugs. You will have no trouble getting a sufficient number of students who want to have a special curriculum, and a special curriculum on mind-altering drugs, ones with either the pharmacology or psychiatry departments. Both of those disciplines are relatively irrelevant to problems of human sexuality and drug use and misuse in American society.
>
> Each of you should go back to your law and medical schools and help to establish a special curriculum on human sexuality and a special curriculum on mind-altering drugs, ones with student involvement and student leadership. You should enlist the aid of persons from all disciplines, not just from the medical ones. You should get them from sociology, criminology, and local programs which have nothing to do with academics or government.   *Joel Fort*

I do not think a special curriculum is necessary.

What I have heard is a lot of rhetoric. I am involved in a free clinic in Philadelphia. How many students from Jefferson show up down there and participate? I sent a letter to every resident and intern on the entire Jefferson house staff, 200 new physicians, and got one volunteer to come to the clinic.

You are talking about something that people do not seem to want to do; they only want to talk about it. If you want to do something, you have got to go out and do it.

We started the free clinic. We did not ask where it was so that we could go help. We started it. It was just that simple. If you want something you have to get up and do it. No one is going to wait around for you to come to them.   *Sidney H. Schnoll*

I was confused when I got to medical school, because I was expecting to see persons who were really involved with others. But the persons in my class sat around and did nothing until someone told them that their spring vacation was coming at an inappropriate time and that they were going to have four days of classes in between exams and then four more days of classes before the vacation. They got up and roared about it. But, when someone wanted to change a new class we have which is called "Medicine in Society," the only thing my classmates wanted to do was boycott the final exam because they thought the class was a farce and should be thrown out.

We are talking a lot, hearing what we want to hear, and applauding it. But what are we doing?

Do not make the error of thinking that persons can be instantly mobilized into hasty and perhaps ill-conceived action. It takes a long time and we do not know what seeds were planted at the drug-abuse symposium. I feel that there was great hope and strength, and that many of the things discussed will get done.   *Lisa A. Richette*